THE NEWBERY
PRACTITIONER'S
GUIDE

THE NEWBERY PRACTITIONER'S GUIDE

MAKING THE MOST OF THE AWARD IN YOUR WORK

edited by **Laura Schulte-Cooper**

Association for Library Service to Children (ALSC)

ALA Editions
CHICAGO | 2022

LAURA SCHULTE-COOPER is the program officer for communications for the Association for Library Service to Children, a division of the American Library Association.

THE ASSOCIATION FOR LIBRARY SERVICE TO CHILDREN (ALSC) is driven by more than four thousand members dedicated to the support and enrichment of library service to children. Our members include youth librarians, literature experts, publishers, and educational faculty. ALSC supports its members in engaging communities to build healthy, successful futures for all children.

Extensive effort has gone into ensuring the reliability of the information in this book; however, the publisher makes no warranty, express or implied, with respect to the material contained herein.

ISBN: 978-0-8389-3827-0 (paper)

Library of Congress Cataloging-in-Publication Data
Names: Schulte-Cooper, Laura, editor. | Association for Library Service to Children, editor.
Title: The Newbery practitioner's guide : making the most of the award in your work / edited by Laura Schulte-Cooper; Association for Library Service to Children.
Description: Chicago : ALA Editions, 2022. | Includes bibliographical references and index. | Summary: "This guide explores the Newbery Award where it intersects with library collection policy, advocacy, programming, EDI efforts, and censorship, among other areas. The guide provides guidance and strategies for library workers serving youth and other adults working with children and literature, to inform and support the work they do involving the Newbery Award"—Provided by publisher.
Identifiers: LCCN 2021062371 | ISBN 9780838938270 (paperback)
Subjects: LCSH: Newbery Medal. | Children's libraries—Collection development—United States. | Children's libraries—Activity programs—United States. | Libraries—Special collections—Children's literature.
Classification: LCC Z718.2.U6 N49 2022 | DDC 025.2/187625—dc23/eng/20220308
LC record available at https://lccn.loc.gov/2021062371

Text design by Kim Hudgins in the Skolar Pro, Rustica, and Brix Slab typefaces. Cover design by Alejandra Diaz; cover image © Adobe Stock.

♾ This paper meets the requirements of ANSI/NISO Z39.48-1992 (Permanence of Paper).

Printed in the United States of America

26 25 24 23 22   5 4 3 2 1

CONTENTS

PREFACE

THE NEWBERY AWARD CELEBRATES ITS ONE HUNDREDTH ANNIVERSARY IN 2021–22. Holding a place for so long on the American literary landscape, it's no wonder that the award is recognized by so many, inside and outside of the library profession. But what does the average library practitioner know about the award beyond gold and silver foil stickers, good book recommendations, and a flurry of mock election results in January? *The Newbery Practitioner's Guide: Making the Most of the Award in Your Work* explores the Newbery Award where it intersects with library collection policy, advocacy, programming, EDI efforts, and censorship, among other areas.

The guide provides background, guidance, and strategies for library workers serving youth and other adults who share children's literature with kids. To set the stage, the introduction serves up nuts-and-bolts details and a behind-the-scenes look at the Newbery Award. Readers will explore key elements of the weeding process, in chapter 1, that are the sound basis for determining whether a Newbery book remains in the library's collection. Chapter 2 surveys where the century-old Newbery Award stands in terms of recognizing racially diverse literature and shares teaching suggestions for a sampling of Newbery titles by authors of color. Examining challenges to past Newbery winners, in chapter 3, readers will learn why specific titles were challenged or banned and gain practical tips for dealing with controversy around award winners. Practitioners will take away from chapter 4 a bounty of activities and group discussion questions designed to help them immerse young readers in thirty-six diverse Newbery titles. Chapter 5 highlights ways to promote the Newbery Award and its winners through booklists and displays, mock elections, bookstagramming, and other opportunities. The final chapter demonstrates ways in which the Newbery Award can be leveraged to raise awareness of the expertise of library workers serving youth and of the wealth of resources available at the library. The Conclusion wraps up with insights on the power of the Newbery Award, teachable moments and social justice connections, and the next hundred years of the award.

The ultimate goal of *The Newbery Practitioner's Guide: Making the Most of the Award in Your Work* is to bring fresh ideas, new perspectives, and additional resources to library workers serving young people and other adults working with children and literature, to inform and support the work they do involving the Newbery Award. We hope this guide helps you make the most of the Newbery.

ACKNOWLEDGMENTS

THE NEWBERY AWARD HISTORY IS LONG, AND IT IS IMPOSSIBLE TO RECOG-nize all those who have carried the award to this hundred-year milestone. There is, however, one definite place to begin: Frederic G. Melcher, American publisher, bookseller, and editor, proposed the John Newbery Medal at an American Library Association (ALA) meeting of the Children's Librarians' Section in June 1921. His idea was heartily accepted by the children's librarians, and the official proposal was approved by the ALA Executive Board in 1922. Without the foresight of Melcher and members of ALA's Children's Librarians' Section, we would not be celebrating the centennial of the Newbery Award nor presenting this publication today.

Also to be gratefully acknowledged are the ALSC members who reviewed an early, rough overview and table of contents for this publication and provided valuable feedback and ideas: Steven Engelfried, Roxanne Feldman, Krishna Grady, Maeve Visser Knoth, Claudette McLinn, Jonda C. McNair, Angela Moffett, Mary Schreiber, and Beatriz Pascual Wallace.

Our volunteer authors gave generously of their time, expertise, and personal experience to build this robust collection of Newbery resources and tools: Ramona Caponegro, Cassie Chenoweth, Jared S. Crossley, Denise Dávila, Alpha Selene DeLap, Lora DeWalt, Steven Engelfried, Kimberly Probert Grad, Jonda C. McNair, Jamie Campbell Naidoo, Pat R. Scales, and Megan Schliesman.

Jamie Santoro, senior acquisitions editor for ALA Editions/ALA Neal-Schuman, provided vital advice, ideas, and support throughout the editorial process. Special thanks also goes to all those ALSC members who have served on the Newbery Award Selection Committee. With their work, commitment, and care, the award has been able to grow and flourish over the past century.

INTRODUCTION

The Nuts and Bolts of the Newbery Award

STEVEN ENGELFRIED

IN 1922, *THE STORY OF MANKIND* BY HENDRIK WILLEM VAN LOON WAS announced as the winner of a new book award: the John Newbery Medal. A century later, the Newbery stands as one of literature's most prestigious and important awards. The gold and silver seals that mark the medal and honor books guide countless readers, young and old, to explore the finest achievements in writing for children. And the Newbery Award is used by countless librarians, teachers, and others who work with children as part of their essential work of inspiring young readers.

The Newbery's Reach

My first encounter with the Newbery came as an eleven-year-old when I noticed those impressive seals (one silver, one gold) on two of the book covers in Lloyd Alexander's Chronicles of Prydain series. Personally, I would have given the gold medal to all of them, but as a child reader there was some satisfaction in knowing that my own favorites were also highly valued by others. At the time, though, I had no idea who those "others" were or how they made their decisions.

A couple decades later, as a children's librarian, I began recommending those Newbery books. The list of winners provided a rich and varied selection of titles, while the seal on the cover helped the child, or sometimes the parent, recognize that this was a quality recommendation. Later, I read many Newbery titles aloud to my own children. Not all were a great fit. *Mrs. Frisby and the Rats of NIMH* and *The Westing Game* were right up their alley; *Smoky the Cowhorse* not so much. Eventually I was fortunate enough to serve on a couple Newbery committees myself, where I learned firsthand about the intense effort and emotional investment every committee puts into the process before finally selecting the winners.

In all of those experiences runs the common thread: there is a standard for excellence in children's books, and when you see that gold or silver seal, you are reading a book that has been deemed "distinguished" by a group of people who made that selection with great care and seriousness.

The Newbery Mission

That was Frederic G. Melcher's intention when he conceived of the award a century ago, at a time when the literary quality of children's books was not widely recognized. Melcher, an American publisher and bookseller, believed this new award could aid librarians in their role of "encouraging the joy of reading among children."[1] The Newbery was the first award for children's literature, but since then dozens of major awards have been established, including the Caldecott Medal in 1938. For many years the Newbery and Caldecott Medals were chosen by a single committee, with discussions and balloting accomplished through mail correspondence. Over the years, the procedures by which members select the winner have evolved, but the mission continues to be as important and as challenging as it was in the beginning: to select the most distinguished children's book of the year.

The Newbery Process: Behind the Scenes

Currently the Newbery committee is made up of fifteen dedicated members who spend a full year with children's books: reading, discussing, and thinking about them, and finally selecting the winner of the John Newbery Medal. The Newbery Manual provides details about how the committee is formed. A completely new group of individuals serves on the committee each year.

The Newbery Terms and Criteria provide guidance for the committee process. Some parts of the criteria are straightforward: authors must be "citizens or residents of the United States,"[2] for instance, which rules out J. K. Rowling and many other excellent authors. Other directions can be more challenging to follow. For example, members are "not to consider . . . whether the author has previously won the award."[3] This means they can't dismiss a book by Jacqueline

Woodson because she's already won four honor awards or over-rate it because it seems like she is long overdue to win the medal.

While the Newbery is for children's books, not everyone realizes that "children are defined as persons of ages up to and including fourteen."[4] This explains how an expertly written picture book such as *Last Stop on Market Street* by Matt de la Peña can win a medal, while Renée Watson's *Piecing Me Together*, a realistic novel about a seventeen-year-old-student, also can earn Newbery recognition. The criteria make it clear that the Newbery is "for literary quality. . . . The award is not for . . . popularity."[5] Katherine Applegate's *The One and Only Ivan* may get read by far more young readers than *Good Masters! Sweet Ladies!* by Laura Amy Schlitz, but both works represent the highest level of artistic excellence that the award demands.

Each year's Newbery committee must apply these integral and wide-ranging terms and criteria to a completely new set of books, and members compare only the titles eligible in that given year. The result is a high-quality list that represents excellence in many styles aimed at a wide variety of readers.

Yet, despite the time and thought invested in the process, evolving literary styles, shifting publishing trends, and cultural changes make it inevitable that award-winning titles that shone in their own time might become less relevant, or even be deemed inappropriate by modern standards. Some Newbery winners—discussed, considered, and chosen so carefully as the best books of their time—aren't necessarily the best of all time.

Even with that in mind, the high standards and stellar reputation of the Newbery Medal still provide unique opportunities for teachers, librarians, parents, and other adults to connect kids with children's books of the highest quality. Just as Frederic G. Melcher envisioned it one hundred years ago.

NOTES

1. Irene Smith, *A History of the Newbery and Caldecott Medals* (New York: Viking Press, 1957), 36.
2. "Terms and Criteria," ALSC, January 16, 2008, www.ala.org/alsc/awardsgrants/bookmedia/newbery.
3. "Terms and Criteria."
4. "Terms and Criteria."
5. "Terms and Criteria."

Weeding and Maintenance of Your Newbery Collection

Meeting the Needs and Interests of Your Library Community

MEGAN SCHLIESMAN

WEEDING AT ITS MOST FUNDAMENTAL DEMANDS LIBRARIANS CONSIDER two questions: 1) Who is the collection I'm responsible for maintaining for? 2) Does this book (or other material) serve that population? But anyone who's spent time weeding knows it's never quite that simple.

The Newbery Award is the oldest and, in many contexts, the best-known children's literature award in the United States. It is revered in our field as a children's literature institution, and that sense of reverence sometimes has an outsized influence on collection development decisions.

If the call to keep older Newbery books seems like an easy one—they're Newbery books after all!—think again. The relevance of past winners and honor books to a contemporary public or school library collection serving youth and families today should not be solely determined by a book's status as a Newbery.

The annual announcement of the Newbery Award, along with other children's literature awards, is met with keen interest and excitement within and even beyond our profession. But librarians understand that every just-announced Newbery won't be a good fit for every collection. For example, because Newbery committees consider books with an audience through age fourteen, some Newbery titles are likely considered out of the scope of most K–4 or K–5 collections, such as the 2018 Newbery Honor Book *Piecing Me Together* by Renée Watson, or the 2013 Newbery Honor Book *Bomb: The Race to Build—and Steal—The World's Most Dangerous Weapon* by Steve Sheinkin.

Decisions about whether to purchase just-announced Newbery titles not already in a collection should be made following board-approved policies and procedures and their stated selection criteria. These typically include consideration of multiple factors, including age recommendations in reviews and collection priorities in light of budget. While interest in specific awards, such as the Newbery, may also be called out, it's a process that must be done book by book by book, and library by library. That, after all, is what collection development demands: making selection decisions that meet the needs and interests of the community a library serves, following the institution's collection development policy, guidelines, and criteria.

Weeding is no different. Yet once a Newbery title is on the shelf, with that oh-so-recognizable gold or silver seal image on the cover proudly proclaiming its status, the eventual decision of whether to weed it can be rife with complications.

Older Newbery Books and Contemporary Collections

Unless a library has a stated goal to collect books considered significant in the history of children's literature, has a research collection for this purpose, and has included Newbery books among those it wants to collect—unlikely for most if not all contemporary school and most public library collections—then the intersection of collection development work and Newbery books is not "maintaining a Newbery collection" but rather determining which Newbery books remain relevant to the youth and families the library serves because no book has a place in a contemporary public or school library collection in perpetuity. To that end, every collection development policy should include additional criteria for weeding, and once a Newbery book is in a collection, it eventually will need to be considered for weeding *just like every other book.*

Like decisions about acquiring a book, decisions about weeding are typically made based on multiple criteria outlined in the policy. These may include whether a book is still in significant demand (usually determined by circulation statistics), whether it is worn (in which case it may be replaced if there is still demonstrated demand, but replacement should not be automatic, even if it's a Newbery title), and whether the content is dated or outdated in some way (more on that in a bit). The policy may reference the helpful *CREW: A Weeding Manual for Modern Libraries* publication and method.

Even with the guidance provided in the policy, decisions about weeding any book, let alone a Newbery title, can be challenging, especially if some adults making selection and weeding decisions have strong nostalgic or sentimental ties to some titles. Nostalgia and sentiment are feelings, not retention criteria, but being clear-eyed about collection development is never harder than when strong feelings, negative or positive, get in the way. Fond memories of reading *Caddie Woodlawn* as a child isn't a factor any librarian should use in determining whether the 1936 Newbery winner belongs in the collection they are managing for children and/or families today. As author Padma Venkatraman notes, "When we defend classics, we're sometimes just defending childhood memories."[1] As professionals, we have to be able to set those memories and the feelings that come with them aside.

When it comes to the Newbery Award, there is also the sense of reverence that can extend from individual books to the award itself. In fact, positive feelings about the award may be the only thing we bring to our evaluation of a Newbery title we've never read—all we know is it won the Newbery. There's that gold seal image on the cover of the 1958 winner *Rifles for Watie* to prove it. But when older Newbery titles are retained simply because they are Newbery titles, we are not only likely ignoring our institution's multifaceted criteria for collection development and weeding, but we are also perpetuating a cycle of reverence that serves no one, least of all the contemporary children and families our libraries serve.

Nostalgia, sentiment, and reverence aren't exclusive to librarians. Parents and grandparents may think longingly of the books they read and enjoyed or even just remember from childhood, and they might expect the public library in particular to be able to provide them. If someone in your community expresses a desire to find *Hitty, Her First Hundred Years* on the shelf, do you purchase the 1930 Newbery winner if you don't have it? The fact that Newbery books often remain in print—perhaps reissued with contemporary covers— means you likely can replace worn copies, or purchase an older Newbery book you don't own, but that doesn't mean you automatically have to, or should.

In a public library in particular, patron requests may play a role in the decision about whether to acquire or retain a title, or replace a worn book, but ideally ongoing circulation statistics (in the case of replacement), the level of demand, and other collection criteria are also stated in the policy as factors to consider in determining whether such requests are filled. The title may be available elsewhere and obtained through interlibrary loan, for example. Similarly, retaining a title because someone *might* request it someday, rather than making collection decisions based on what you know about meeting the needs and interests of the youth and families you serve, makes little sense. Weeding is not a "What if" activity (i.e., "What if someone wants this someday?").

Of course, there are older Newbery titles that continue to captivate readers today and may merit inclusion in many contemporary collections, even if the number of copies in demand may gradually wane, and their appeal won't necessarily be consistent in every community or school (nor, likely, has it ever been). The 1953 Newbery Honor Book *Charlotte's Web*, 1963 winner *A Wrinkle in Time*, 1968 winner *From the Mixed-Up Files of Mrs. Basil E. Frankweiler*, 1977 winner *Roll of Thunder, Hear My Cry*, and 1979 winner *The Westing Game* are all examples of older Newbery books that continue to capture the imagination of at least some contemporary readers.

Representation Matters

Eliminating nostalgia and a sense of reverence means evaluating Newbery books on their own merits in terms of the needs and interests of contemporary collections and the young readers they serve. Those readers are not all white; in many places they never have been, yet for decades an assumption of whiteness was the default thinking in our white-dominated profession and in publishing regarding readers of children's literature, and no doubt the same is true for many Newbery committees. We all have been learning to expand our understanding, and with it our critical thinking, thanks in large part to the work of librarians and others who are Black, Indigenous, and people of color.

Respect for all readers demands we be clear-eyed about the Newbery Award and its history, including problematic representation, which doesn't serve any child, regardless of race. Respect for the award demands this, too.

Newbery Award books across the years reflect dominant attitudes about race, ethnicity, specific cultures, and gender at the time they were written. This absolutely matters when it comes to the relevance of past Newbery titles in collections for contemporary children and families. Regardless of when they were written, words matter. And make no mistake: A Newbery book that is racist, such as the 1923 winner *The Voyages of Doctor Dolittle*, was always racist, even if too many of us didn't understand this for far too long.

There isn't a shortage of examples of Newbery books with questionable representation, from the previously mentioned *Caddie Woodlawn* to 1961 winner *Island of the Blue Dolphins*, 1974 winner *The Slave Dancer*, 1984 Newbery Honor Book *The Sign of the Beaver*, and others. In evaluating older Newbery books for weeding, it's critical to consider concerns about representation in light of weeding criteria that may help guide decision-making. Criteria such as "dated," "outdated," and "timeliness" all have relevance when considering older Newbery titles for contemporary collections. So, too, does any language in a selection policy regarding materials with racism and sexism—sometimes found in school library policies in particular, in language such as "materials free from stereotype or bias."

Non-quantitative weeding (and selection) criteria are inevitably open to interpretation. Interrogating how we understand and apply them is critical. Is a book outdated, for example, if it reflects decades-old dominant culture attitudes that we now understand to be racist? On the one hand, nothing about the book has changed; on the other, our understanding—as individuals, as a profession, and as a society—has changed. One hopes the answer is yes.

Still, weeding, like selection, involves weighing various criteria as outlined in policies and procedures to arrive at a decision. In the case of concerns about representation, determining that a book is dated because of racist images reflecting outdated ideas may be the most significant factor in deciding whether a book still belongs in the collection supporting the curriculum and/or the needs and interests of contemporary children and families. But other factors are likely to play a role, most notably demand. In public libraries in particular, patron demand and circulation statistics may be prioritized, so books that are still circulating well are likely to remain, although it's possible the number of copies in place exceeds what is necessary. School libraries may have more latitude depending on policy language and the scope of their mission and collection goals.

What's important is that if a book does remain, it will be in the collection for a reason that goes beyond the fact it is a Newbery title.

Finally, it's always important to remember that even if a book remains on the shelf based on selection and weeding criteria, it's critical to use professional judgment when it comes to choosing—and not choosing—materials to highlight in programming, displays, and other ways.

A Few Words about Intellectual Freedom and Censorship

Intellectual freedom is a foundational value in our profession. But it's important to remember that intellectual freedom has never meant libraries buy or keep everything. And along with the values we celebrate and the rights we uphold comes the responsibility we have to professionally curate our collections following board-approved policies and procedures.

When it comes to curating collections, collection development and weeding go hand in hand. As librarians Mary Kelly and Holly Hibner write on their website, Awful Library Books (Hoarding Is Not Collection Development), "Weeding is necessary to remain relevant to our users and true to our missions ... unless your library exists to archive and preserve materials for the ages, we are not in the business of collecting physical things. We collect information and provide access to information."[2]

The goal of most school and public library youth collection development work is to maintain a collection relevant to contemporary readers. Doing so requires weighing multiple factors as outlined in a library's mission, goals, and collection criteria. While some degree of subjectivity is impossible to avoid, when weeding (and acquisition) are done following an institution's policies and procedures, and criteria are applied as consistently as possible, then rest assured that it is weeding, not censorship, even if some decisions are not always easy or clear-cut.

Ultimately, the two essential questions remain: Who is this collection for? Does this material serve them?

Beyond the Book
ADDITIONAL RESOURCES/READINGS

Larson, Jeanette. *CREW: A Weeding Manual for Modern Libraries.* Revised and updated by Jeanette Larson. Austin: Texas State Library and Archives Commission, 2012.

Tate, Binnie Wilkin. *African and African American Images in Newbery Award Winning Titles: Progress in Portrayals.* Lanham, MD: Scarecrow Press, 2010.

NOTES

1. Padma Venkatraman, "Weeding Out Racism: Challenging Old Classics Is Akin to Replacing Racist Statues," *School Library Journal* 66, no. 8 (August 2020): 22.

2. Mary Kelly and Holly Hibner, "Why We Weed," AwfulLibraryBooks.net, https://awfullibrarybooks.net/why-weed/.

The Newbery
in a Changing World

The Recognition of Racially Diverse Literature

JONDA C. MCNAIR AND JARED S. CROSSLEY

AS SOMEONE WHO SPECIALIZES IN AND IS PASSIONATE ABOUT CHILDREN'S
literature, a professional highlight for me (Jonda) each year is attending the
Youth Media Awards announcements during the ALA Midwinter Meeting.
This typically has entailed getting up at the crack of dawn, standing in a long
line while debating and discussing predictions about award winners with
other ALSC members, and then, eventually, filing into a large auditorium to
await the announcements. It is exhilarating to be seated with my ALSC colleagues, especially my close book-loving friends, as we excitedly wait for the
ceremony to begin, then cheer for books we love and our friends who are serving on committees as their names appear on the screen. Because the Newbery
Medal is ALSC's oldest and arguably most prestigious award, the winners (and
the Caldecott Medal winners) are always announced last during the ceremony.
There is typically a statement that goes something like this: "And now, for the
announcement of ALA's oldest and most widely known awards. . . ."

I have been attending the Youth Media Awards ceremonies annually since
I served on the Coretta Scott King Award jury in 2008, not long after I became
an ALSC member in 2005. Until the last eight years or so, the majority of books
written by and about people of color announced during the ceremony were
generally recipients of awards created specifically for people of color, such as
the Pura Belpré and the Coretta Scott King. It was oftentimes not unusual to
see no authors of color at all recognized in a given year for the Newbery Medal.

In an editorial published in 1996 titled "A Wider Vision for the Newbery," Parravano and Adams wrote,

> [A]n examination of the fiction medalists over the past ten years . . . quickly disperses any idea of diversity. All are middle-grade novels; all are by white authors and feature white protagonists (Salamanca Tree Hiddle's great-great-grandmother notwithstanding). The last author from a parallel culture to win the Newbery Medal was Mildred Taylor for *Roll of Thunder, Hear My Cry* (Dial) in 1977. While several honor awards have been given to nonwhite authors since 1986, the big prize has, for almost twenty years now, been out of reach.[1]

Similarly, in an article published in 1998, Miller wrote,

> When for twenty-one years a body of literature with the power of the Newbery gold lacks even one text by a minority writer or about a minority lead, the message sent to children is that the "most distinguished" protagonists and authors are white.[2]

However, in 2015 with the announcement of *The Crossover* by Kwame Alexander as winner of the Newbery Medal, there was a seismic shift in regard to authors of color being recognized on a consistent basis each year. In addition, that year, two Newbery Honor titles were chosen, and one of them was *Brown Girl Dreaming* by Jacqueline Woodson, meaning that two-thirds of the titles selected in 2015 were written by and about African Americans. What follows in this chapter is first a brief history of the Newbery Medal in regard to the recognition of authors of color from its inception in 1922 up until recently, with a particular focus on the recent consistent representation of authors of color since 2015. (Please note, this historical information is based on what is publicly available in regard to authors' racial identities.) Second, we focus on possible explanations for this recent consistent recognition of authors of color while incorporating insights from a number of prominent ALSC members, including librarians and publishing representatives. Finally, we conclude with a focus on the progress that has been made recently and the need to continue the important work of promoting and paying attention to books written by and about people of color. To round out the chapter, at the end, we include teaching suggestions for a small sampling of Newbery books by authors of color.

The Newbery Award and Its History in Regard to Recognizing Authors of Color

When Kwame Alexander was recognized in 2015 for *The Crossover*, it had been fifteen years since another African American, Christopher Paul Curtis, received the Newbery Medal in 2000 for *Bud, Not Buddy*. I wondered how many people of color would be recognized the following year or if it would be another fifteen years before an African American would win the medal again. In order to understand my apprehension, it is necessary to consider the history of the Newbery Medal and its recognition of authors of color. The award was established in 1922, and Dhan Gopal Mukerji was the first author of color who won the Newbery Medal, in 1928 for a book titled *Gay-Neck: The Story of a Pigeon*. Although Arna Bontemps received a Newbery Honor in 1949 for *Story of the Negro*, it would not be until 1975, more than fifty years after the creation of the award, that an African American, Virginia Hamilton, would win the Newbery Medal for her novel *M.C. Higgins, the Great*. Over the course of her career, Hamilton also earned three Newbery Honors (in 1972, 1983, and 1989). Mildred D. Taylor was the second African American to win the Newbery Medal, in 1977 for the classic *Roll of Thunder, Hear My Cry*.

Paula Fox, whose mother was Cuban, won the Newbery Medal in 1974 for *The Slave Dancer*, which features a white character who plays music for slaves. The book was later criticized for inaccuracies about the Black experience by organizations such as the Council on Interracial Books for Children.[3] In 2016, Matt de la Peña won the Newbery Medal for his picture book *Last Stop on Market Street*. Meg Medina won in 2019 for *Merci Suárez Changes Gears*. And, in 2022, Donna Barba Higuera won for *The Last Cuentista*, making her the fourth Latinx author to win the Newbery Medal. Before 2016, only Paula Fox had won the Newbery Medal, although Margarita Engle won a Newbery Honor in 2009 for *The Surrender Tree: Poems of Cuba's Struggle for Freedom*. After Mukerji's *Gay-Neck: The Story of a Pigeon*, Linda Sue Park's *A Single Shard* was the next title by an Asian American to win the Newbery Medal, in 2002, followed by Cynthia Kadohata in 2005 for *Kira-Kira*. It should be noted that Laurence Yep received two Newbery Honors, for *Dragonwings* and *Dragon's Gate*, both of which are considered classics. In 1978, Jamake Highwater, who claimed Native ancestry, received a Newbery Honor for *Anpao: An American Indian Odyssey*. He was exposed in 1984 as a fraud in an investigative report by Hank Adams in *Akwesasne Notes* and by Jack Anderson in the *Washington Post*.[4] As of 2022, however, there is now one Native author, to our knowledge, to be awarded a Newbery Honor. Darcie Little Badger of the Lipan Apache Tribe received a 2022 Newbery Honor for *A Snake Falls to Earth*. From 2015 to 2022, seven of the eight winners of the Newbery Medal were authors of color: two African Americans, two Asian Americans, and three Latin Americans. This is in stark contrast to the history, before 2015, of authors of color being recognized by the Newbery Award Selection Committee.

Possible Explanations for the Consistent and Recent Recognition of Authors of Color

There are several explanations for this phenomenon. After reaching out to ALSC members (e.g., former ALSC presidents, chairs of ALSC award committees, editors), a number of interesting possible reasons emerged for the consistent and recent recognition of authors of color. Diversifying book award committees was listed by several interviewees as a key factor. When asked for his thoughts about the increased number of Newbery Medals being awarded to authors of color, former ALSC President Jamie Campbell Naidoo wrote,

> [P]erhaps the most influential reason . . . is the increase in persons of color on award selection committees. More diversity at the table allows for richer conversations and provides momentum in discussions about culturally authentic stories that resonate with children from diverse ethnic, racial, and other cultural backgrounds—not just the default white reader.[5]

Likewise, when presented with this same question, Nina Lindsay, another former ALSC president and the 2008 Newbery Award Selection Committee chair, wrote, "I'm sure it has to do with the presence of more BIPOC [black, Indigenous, and people of color] members on the committees, and—perhaps even more so—in our critical conversations at large."[6] Deborah Taylor, who served on the 2002 Newbery Award Selection Committee, wrote, "While we are nowhere near where we would like to be, the focused attention of ALSC to have more diversity on its committees is a factor as is the efforts of review sources to diversify their reviewers."[7] Even an increasing number of Newbery Award Selection Committee chairs have been people of color. For example, the 2020 (Krishna Grady), 2021 (Jonda C. McNair), and 2023 (Christina Vortia) chairs are African American women.

Lindsay also noted that she believes history has strongly impacted the selection of books and led some committee members to think of a certain type of book that is worthy of the Newbery Medal: "[A]s long as there is a lack of diversity in previously recognized titles—in style, in subject matter, in characters, etc.—many people tend to think of a 'type' of Newbery book."[8] Perhaps with the increase in winning books by people of color, the notion of what a Newbery winner should be (and who it is written by and about) is shifting. Kathleen T. Horning wrote,

> In the children's book world, awards matter a great deal. . . . And they have always had a big impact on what gets published next. Success breeds imitation, so when authors and illustrators of color win book awards, particularly the Newbery and Caldecott Medals, it can lead to greater diversity in literature overall.[9]

Taylor, along with others, also noted the impact of the We Need Diverse Books (WNDB) movement: "The rise of social media, and that includes WNDB since it started as a hashtag on Twitter, has increased dialogue and brought voices in from outside the library profession and encouraged those within to examine their biases."[10] Likewise, Cecilia McGowan, a former ALSC president and the 2018 Newbery Award Selection Committee chair, wrote,

> I think We Need Diverse Books has helped the effort, not only in helping publishers understand how much we need these books, but also as a way for everyone (parents, teachers, librarians, general public) to understand how they are valuable to/for all of us.[11]

In addition, Taylor highlighted the role of awards such as the Coretta Scott King, Pura Belpré, and Asian/Pacific American awards: "I do think the years of advocacy from CSK [Coretta Scott King], Belpr[é], etc. have had an effect in terms of more exposure and acceptance of diverse titles and authors."[12] We would argue that these awards have brought numerous authors to the attention of all librarians, thereby introducing them to the larger children's book world. For example, Jacqueline Woodson, Rita Williams-Garcia, and Jason Reynolds, all of whom have earned at least one Newbery Honor, were recipients of the Coretta Scott King Award first. In addition, similar to other interviewees, Naidoo noted that "children's library professionals are engaging more in conversations around cultural humility and cultural competence, broadening their receptiveness to diverse stories" by authors of color.[13] ALSC, for example, has made a strong commitment to diversity, equity, and inclusion, making these a key component of its 2020–2023 strategic plan.[14]

Finally, related to the increase in authors of color being consistently recognized by the Newbery recently, another common factor noted by several interviewees was a rise in the number of diverse authors being published. Kirby McCurtis, a former ALSC president and a member of the 2018 Newbery Award Selection Committee, wrote, "I think it is a matter of more available titles from publishers of all sizes getting into the hands of the committee members."[15] Naidoo commented, "there is an increased awareness in the children's book industry towards publishing more diverse titles representative of all children, particularly titles written by those with lived cultural experiences."[16] For example, statistics collected by the Cooperative Children's Book Center show that there were 108 books (received by the center) published in 2015 by Black/African authors and 60 by Latinx authors. In 2020, there were 252 books (received by the center) published by Black/African authors and 228 books by Latinx authors.[17] Phoebe Yeh, an editor of children's and young adult authors such as Kwame Alexander, Eloise Greenfield, and Walter Dean Myers, wrote,

> Big children's publishers such as Penguin Random House and Harper-Collins create imprints that publish only BIPOC books. At Random House Children's Books, we start keeping track of our diverse titles and authors. We are publishing more BIPOC books. My own list at Crown Books for Young Readers has shifted as a reflection of the submissions, now almost all BIPOC debut authors.[18]

One example of an imprint that Yeh referred to is Heartdrum, HarperCollins's imprint for titles by Native and First Nations authors and illustrators.

Conclusion

The recognition of authors of color by the Newbery Award Selection Committee on a consistent basis has been a long time in coming, and we hope the trend of inclusive Newbery Medal and Honor winners continues. We believe that this phenomenon is due to a confluence of factors, which we highlighted in this chapter. Classroom teachers and librarians can also make a difference by integrating and using Newbery Medal and Honor titles by authors of color all year long and advocating to parents, colleagues, principals, and others why children need distinguished books that will be mirrors, windows, and sliding glass doors for them.[19]

Teaching Suggestions with a Sampling of Newbery Titles by Authors of Color

Bud, Not Buddy by Christopher Paul Curtis (New York: Delacorte, 1999)

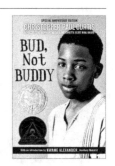

MEDAL WINNER, 2000

A ten-year-old orphan named Bud travels across Michigan, from Flint to Grand Rapids, during the Great Depression in search of a man he believes is his father.

Discussion Questions

1. What do you know about the Great Depression? What stories have some of your family members told regarding what they remember about this time period?
2. Several books by Christopher Paul Curtis, such as *The Watsons Go to Birmingham—1963* and *Elijah of Buxton*, are historical fiction. What are the characteristics of this genre, and why do you think the author may have chosen to set his stories in the past?
3. What was your favorite scene from *Bud, Not Buddy*, and why?

Activities

1. Bud travels across Michigan, from Flint to Grand Rapids. Find a map of the state and determine how many miles Bud travels to search for his father. Compare the technological resources (e.g., Google Maps, Siri) that you have now with what Bud would have had available to him in the 1930s.
2. Bud creates "Bud Caldwell's Rules and Things for Having a Funner Life and Making a Better Liar Out of Yourself." Rule 328 is "When You Make Up Your Mind to Do Something, Hurry Up and Do It, If You Wait You Might Talk Yourself Out of What You Wanted in the First Place." Make a rule book for yourself and then give it a title and illustrate the cover. What are some of the rules you would create to guide yourself through life?
3. Read other books (e.g., *Esperanza Rising* by Pam Muñoz Ryan, *Out of the Dust* by Karen Hesse) in which characters are living during the Great Depression, and compare the settings, characters, and plotlines using

Venn diagrams. Consider how the varying racial identities (e.g., African American, Latinx, white) of the characters in the books impacted their experiences and their treatment during this era.

Echo by Pam Muñoz Ryan (New York: Scholastic, 2015)
HONOR BOOK, 2016

An enchanted harmonica travels through Nazi Germany and across the ocean to the United States, intertwining the lives of four children and helping them each through their dire circumstances.

Discussion Questions

1. Friedrich, Ivy, and the Yamamoto family are each treated unfairly due to prejudice toward their race or their perceived differences. What are some instances when you witnessed someone being treated unfairly because of their race or physical differences? What can you do to help others if you see this happening to them?
2. The book has the recurring prophecy, "Your fate is not yet sealed. Even in the darkest night, a star will shine, a bell will chime, a path will be revealed." How did you see this prophecy play out in the lives of Otto, Friedrich, Mike, and Ivy?
3. Would you rather conduct a symphony, play in a symphony, or attend a symphony, and why?

Activities

1. The harmonica in *Echo* takes a journey around the world, starting with Otto and Friedrich in Germany. It then travels to Mike in Philadelphia, Pennsylvania, and to Ivy in Fresno, California, then to the Los Angeles area in Southern California. The harmonica then makes its way back to Germany with Kenny Yamamoto. Using a map, track the journey of the harmonica and figure out about how far (in miles) it travels through the story. Have you been to any of the places the harmonica visits in the book? If you could visit one of these places, where would you go, and why?
2. Friedrich talks about being able to listen to music with your heart. Choose a song to listen to that is important to the book, such as "Lullaby" by Johannes Brahms, "Sleeping Beauty Waltz" by Pyotr Ilyich Tchaikovsky, "America the Beautiful," or "Auld Lang Syne" (harmonica

renditions of these songs are available on YouTube). While listening, consider what it means to listen to music with your heart. While the song is playing, create an abstract drawing, using simple shapes, flowing lines, and colors, that is representative of how the song makes you feel. Examples and ideas for basic abstract art can be found online.

3. Part four in the book ends by saying that Ivy, Friedrich, Mike, the rest of the orchestra, and the audience were all "connected by the same silken thread." Using a ball of yarn, make a web. Have everyone get in a circle, and choose someone on the opposite side of the circle from you to compliment. After giving them a compliment, hold on to a loose end of the yarn with one hand and toss the ball to the person you complimented with your other hand. That person then repeats this with someone else across the circle. This continues until everyone in the circle is holding a piece of the yarn, and you are all connected. Talk about how this relates to the message in the book about being connected.

The Undefeated by Kwame Alexander, illus. by Kadir Nelson (Boston: Versify/Houghton Mifflin Harcourt, 2019)

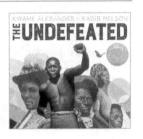

HONOR BOOK, 2020

This poetic tribute to Black America conveys the spirit of resiliency, strength, and bravery that African Americans have embodied throughout US history, including today.

Discussion Questions

1. Which pages or images stood out to you the most? What do you think made this page stand out to you?
2. Did you recognize any of the people shown in this book, and, if so, who? Why do you think this person was included? Which people, or pages, in the book do you want to know more about?
3. How can learning about societal issues and problems such as slavery and racism help improve the world today?

Activities

1. Use the "Historical Figures and Events Featured in *The Undefeated*" section at the back of the book to help guide reports on people or events

highlighted in the text. Have everyone select someone or something portrayed in the book to learn more about. After reading what is written about their topic in the book, have everyone write down additional questions they have about that person or event to investigate further by using the internet or other books. Then, ask everyone to create a presentation (digital or a physical poster) about that individual or historical event.

2. Read the "Afterword" section at the end of the book. Talk about how this book is written as a poem and examine the elements of poetry (e.g., rhythm, repetition) contained in the book. Explore poetry by other African American poets (e.g., Nikki Grimes, Eloise Greenfield, Langston Hughes, Carole Boston Weatherford). Use the "Historical Figures and Events Featured in *The Undefeated*" section to help select a person or historical event and write a poem about that person or event. Invite the sharing of poems, either by reading them orally or hanging them somewhere for display.

3. Conduct an author/illustrator study of the author, Kwame Alexander, or the illustrator, Kadir Nelson. Use their websites and/or social media sites to learn more about them. View or listen to their online interviews. Learn about and read other books that they created and look for patterns or themes across their work. After learning more about the author or illustrator, create a presentation (e.g., video, slides, poster) about Alexander or Nelson. Alternatively, write letters to them to share your thoughts about what you have learned and what you are most interested in about their work.

When You Trap a Tiger by Tae Keller
(New York: Random House Children's Books, 2020)
MEDAL WINNER, 2021

Lily meets a magical, invisible tiger that persuades her to release bottled-up, potentially dangerous stories in an attempt to save Halmoni, Lily's sick grandmother.

Discussion Questions

1. When Lily retells the story about the tiger that eats the grandma, Jensen says, "That sounds like 'Little Red Riding Hood!'" Lily gets defensive, feeling like "this story is completely different. . . . It's

special." Why do you think she doesn't want to compare the traditional folktale with the story she was told by Halmoni?

2. Lily compares the tiger to the strength she sees in the women from her family. If you were to choose an animal to represent one of your family's strengths, which animal would you choose, and why?

Activities

1. Halmoni tells Lily that the stars are actually stories that have been told but that some of these stories are dangerous. The tiger tells Lily that "story magic is powerful, powerful enough to change someone." If possible, observe the night sky full of stars. If not possible, turn out the lights and project a photograph of the night sky full of stars, which can be easily found online. Imagine that each star represents a story. Which of these stories is yours? Have everyone write down a part of their story, something that has happened in their life or in the life of their family.

2. Joe, the librarian, tells Lily that stories "connect continents" and "connect people." Find a short traditional folktale from the country that your family or ancestors are from. Print out or write down the folktales found, fold them up, and put them all into a large, empty jar. Pull several folktales out of the jar and read them aloud. This can be done in one day or over a period of time. Use this as a way to discuss how these folktales can connect people both locally and globally.

3. Joe tells Lily that "stories are like water. Like rain. We can hold them tight, but they always slip through our fingers . . . but remember that water gives us life. . . . And in quiet moments, when the water's still, sometimes we can see our own reflection." Have everyone scoop up some water in their hands and see how it slips out of their hands when they try to hold it tight. How does this relate to stories? Help everyone identify a story in which they can see their own reflection.

Beyond the Book

ADDITIONAL RESOURCES/READINGS

Adichie, Chimamanda Ngozi. "The Danger of a Single Story." July 2009. TED video, 18:33. www.ted.com/talks/chimamanda_ngozi_adichie_the_danger_of_a_single_story.

Beullens-Maoui, Nathalie, and Teresa Mlawer, eds. *The Pura Belpré Award 1996–2016: 20 Years of Outstanding Latino Children's Literature*. Rosen Publishing, 2016.

Bishop, Rudine Sims. *Free Within Ourselves: The Development of African American Children's Literature*. Greenwood Press, 2007.

López-Robertson, Julia. *Celebrating Our Cuentos: Choosing and Using Latinx Literature in Elementary Classrooms*. Scholastic, 2021.

McNair, Jonda C. "#WeNeedMirrorsAndWindows: Diverse Classroom Libraries for K–6 Students." *The Reading Teacher* 70, no. 3 (2016): 375–81. https://doi.org/10.1002/trtr.1516.

Reese, Debbie. "American Indians in Children's Literature." https://americanindiansinchildrensliterature.blogspot.com.

NOTES

1. Martha V. Parravano and Lauren Adams, "A Wider Vision for the Newbery," *The Horn Book Magazine*, January 7, 1996, www.hbook.com/story/a-wider-vision-for-the-newbery-vhe.

2. Bonnie J. F. Miller, "What Color Is Gold? Twenty-One Years of Same-Race Authors and Protagonists in the Newbery Medal," *Journal of Youth Services in Libraries* 12, no. 1 (Fall 1998): 34.

3. Joel Taxel, "The Black Experience in Children's Fiction: Controversies Surrounding Award Winning Books," *Curriculum Inquiry* 16, no. 3 (1986): 245–81, https://doi.org/10.1080/03626784.1986.11076005.

4. Debbie Reese, "Claims to Native Identity in Children's Literature," *American Indian Culture and Research Journal* 43, no. 4 (2019): 123–32, https://doi.org/10.17953/aicrj.43.4.reese.

5. Jamie Campbell Naidoo, e-mail message to author, September 4, 2021.

6. Nina Lindsay, e-mail message to author, September 6, 2021.

7. Deborah Taylor, e-mail message to author, May 28, 2021.

8. Lindsay, e-mail message to author.

9. Kathleen T. Horning, "Milestones for Diversity in Children's Literature and Library Services," *Children & Libraries* 13, no. 3 (Fall 2015): 7, https://doi.org/10.5860/cal.13n3.7.

10. Taylor, e-mail message to author.

11. Cecilia McGowan, e-mail message to author, September 6, 2021.

12. Taylor, e-mail message to author.

13. Naidoo, e-mail message to author.

14. "ALSC 2020–23 Strategic Plan," ALSC, May 28, 2020, www.ala.org/alsc/aboutalsc/stratplan.

15. Kirby McCurtis, e-mail message to author, September 7, 2021.

16. Naidoo, e-mail message to author.

17. "Books by and/or about Black, Indigenous and People of Color (All Years)," Cooperative Children's Book Center, School of Education, University of Wisconsin-Madison, April 16, 2021, https://ccbc.education.wisc.edu/literature-resources/ccbc-diversity-statistics/books-by-about-poc-fnn/.

18. Phoebe Yeh, e-mail message to author, October 12, 2021.

19. Rudine Sims Bishop, "Mirrors, Windows, and Sliding Glass Doors," *Perspectives: Choosing and Using Books for the Classroom* 6, no. 3 (1990): ix–xi.

Challenged and Banned Newbery Books

How to Address Challenges and Deal with Controversial Books

PAT R. SCALES

IN THE EARLY HOURS OF A MIDWINTER MORNING, THE ANNOUNCEMENT OF the Newbery Medal winner and Honor Books takes place at a press conference and is streamed across the internet. Almost immediately news reporters and critics begin publishing their opinions of the winners. Chatter takes place on social media, and people who haven't even read the books weigh in, sometimes causing parents, teachers, and librarians to question whether these "distinguished" books are appropriate for children. This, of course, didn't happen in the early days when there was no press conference, and the winning titles were revealed to the board of directors of ALSC before they were made public. It sometimes took months before the news traveled to librarians and bookstores. And it took even longer before the books got in the hands of children. This doesn't mean that the early winners haven't been marked by controversy; it only means that it took much longer for censors to take notice.

Newbery books have a long history of being challenged, banned, or abridged to remove controversial language. From *The Voyages of Doctor Dolittle* to *The Higher Power of Lucky,* Newbery titles have been challenged for religious reasons, violence, controversial language, and more. This chapter presents many of those titles and the reasons why they set off alarm bells and offers guidance on addressing challenges without censoring and practical ways to deal with controversial books that could eliminate challenges altogether.

Why Was That Newbery Challenged?

It was 1989 before *Amos Fortune, Free Man* by Elizabeth Yates, the 1951 Newbery Medal winner, raised a red flag. Parents in Maryland objected to the book because it has "racist dialogue, fosters stereotypes, and could be degrading to black children." Though *Sounder* by William Armstrong has been quietly "problematic" since it was named the winner in 1970, the first recorded challenge by the American Library Association's (ALA) Office for Intellectual Freedom (OIF) came in 1996 in Rockingham, New York, because of "the word 'nigger' and a reference to the main character, a black sharecropper, as 'boy.'"

There have been incidents of expurgation by publishers, teachers, and librarians. *The Voyages of Doctor Dolittle* by Hugh Lofting, the 1923 Newbery Medal winner, was actually "expurgated in the 1960s by the publisher to make the book conform to the changing sensibilities." Now, most children only know the Disney version of this book.

It was students in Greenville, South Carolina, who noted the removal of content in *My Brother Sam Is Dead*, the 1975 Newbery Honor Book by James and Christopher Collier. As fifth-graders, these students read the book when they studied the American Revolution. Then in middle school they saw that the library book was different than the copies they had used in the classroom. Profanity and some of the violence had been eradicated from the text of paperback copies marketed to classroom teachers.

It's quite possible that children across the nation have noticed blacked-out words in other books, too, like Katherine Paterson's *Bridge to Terabithia* (1978 Newbery Medal) and *The Great Gilly Hopkins* (1979 Newbery Honor Book), and Christopher Paul Curtis' *Bud, Not Buddy* (2000 Newbery Medal). These blacked-out words ignite the curiosity of the young and send them scrabbling to supply their own "uncensored" words. This poses serious questions: What does this practice teach children about censorship? Are they learning that it's okay to take a Sharpie to words and ideas that offend them? How do they learn to become critical thinkers if they aren't allowed to consider the entire book?

It's common for profanity to be questioned in books, but there are many other reasons Newbery books are censored. *The Witch of Blackbird Pond* by Elizabeth George Speare (1959 Newbery Medal), *A Wrinkle in Time* by Madeleine L'Engle (1963 Newbery Medal), *Jacob Have I Loved* by Katherine Paterson (1981 Newbery Medal), *Catherine, Called Birdy* by Karen Cushman (1995 Newbery Honor Book), and Zilpha Keatley Snyder's *The Egypt Game* (1968 Newbery Honor Book), *The Headless Cupid* (1972 Newbery Honor Book), and *The Witches of Worm* (1973 Newbery Honor Book) have been challenged for religious reasons. There are those who don't believe any reference to witchcraft, satanism, and the occult belong in children's books. Neither do they approve of ghoulish books like *The Graveyard Book* by Neil Gaiman, the 2009 medal winner. The committee lauded Gaiman's novel for its "mix of murder, fantasy, humor, and human longing," all out of the realm of understanding to those adults who are self-proclaimed "protectors of children's minds."

Violence in children's books also gives adults pause. *Johnny Tremain* by Esther Forbes (1944 Newbery Medal), *Dragonwings* by Laurence Yep (1976 Newbery Honor Book), and *The Westing Game* by Ellen Raskin (1979 Newbery Medal) have at one time or another been deemed too violent for young readers. *Long Way Down* by Jason Reynolds (2018 Newbery Honor Book), described by the publisher as "an intense snapshot of the chain reaction caused by the pulling of a trigger," has been challenged in the wake of recent incidents of gun violence in the nation. *Abel's Island* by William Steig (1977 Newbery Honor Book) has actually been challenged because there is a "reference to drinking wine." *The Midwife's Apprentice* by Karen Cushman (1996 Newbery Medal) has simply been labeled by some adults as "not appropriate for middle school." No specific reason has been stated.

Soon after Phyllis Reynolds Naylor received the news that *Shiloh* had been named the 1992 Newbery winner, she began receiving complaint letters. One teacher, who was reading the book aloud to a group of fourth-graders, was surprised when she came across the passage where Judd Travers, the villain, uses profanity when he calls his dogs. Why was the teacher reading a book aloud that she hadn't first read herself? Some teachers who read the book aloud openly admit that they skip the word. The editor of the book received a letter from a mother who was troubled by the "bad grammar" in the novel. Set in the mountains of West Virginia, Marty Preston, the book's main character, speaks in Appalachian dialect. The language helps to define the setting, and it's likely the book would not have won the Newbery Medal had it been written in standard English.

The Giver by Lois Lowry was challenged and removed from classrooms in California shortly after the novel was named the 1994 Newbery Medal winner. "Violence and sexual passages" were the reasons cited. The novel ranked eleventh on ALA's list of 100 Most Frequently Challenged Books, 1990–1999. And in 2007, another group of California parents demanded that the book be removed from reading lists because of "adolescent pill-popping, suicide, and lethal injections given to babies and the elderly." Adolescents grasp the themes in this novel and come away pondering what it would be like to live in a society of "sameness." And most can talk intellectually about the cautionary and ethical issues the book raises. The novel was labeled by many critics as "a modern classic." The objections to the book began waning until the 2019 publication of a graphic novel version. A staff member in a public library in Michigan asked that the graphic novel be moved to the adult section because she was so troubled by the content and images in the book. Her request was granted. Many public libraries allow children to use the entire collection, but moving a novel like *The Giver* from the children's room to another area of the library denies young readers ease of access to a book that is intended for them and is considered censorship.

Perhaps the most widely publicized case of censorship of a Newbery winner in the twenty-first century is centered on one word. In a matter of weeks after *The Higher Power of Lucky* by Susan Patron was named the winner in 2007, people criticized the book because on the first page ten-year-old Lucky Trimble overhears Short Sammy say that his dog got bitten on the scrotum by a rattlesnake. It all started when a librarian asked others on LM-Net if they would purchase the book. The word "scrotum" made her nervous. After all "the book is for children," she stated. *The New York Times* (February 18, 2007) ran a story with the headline, "With One Word, Children's Book Sets Off Uproar." Other newspapers sensationalized the story without once asking for an analysis of the book. And no one asked the children whether they knew the meaning of the word, why the word was important to the story, or whether it made them uncomfortable, until the host of an NPR talk show in California asked a ten-year-old girl if she knew what scrotum meant. She answered, in a very matter of fact way, "not at the beginning of the story, but I knew at the end." This young girl recognized what Lucky was searching for all along is a "permanent" mother. A mother she could ask: "What does scrotum mean?" This novel hasn't been the target of censors since the year it was crowned winner. It's unclear whether the issue has blown over, or whether librarians, out of fear, simply don't purchase the book. The latter is a form of professional censorship.

These cases are a few examples of some of the challenges that have been filed against Newbery Medal winners and Honor Books. The people attempting to censor these books are most often parents, but they are also teachers, librarians, and sometimes organized groups with a mission to instill their own values on "all" children by controlling what they read. School and public library administrators who have dealt with censorship in the past also may be tempted to do whatever it takes to avoid public controversy regarding books for youth. However, there are ways to deal with challenges without engaging in professional censorship. If those who challenge books win the censorship war, then eventually there will be no "distinguished books" in libraries.

Newbery Books in the Classroom

One of the reasons that censorship has grown to epidemic levels in schools is because there are more elementary and middle school libraries than in the early days of the Newbery Awards program. Also, in the past, teachers used textbooks to teach literature. Now, once the young become independent readers, teachers are eager to teach them entire novels. And these teachers often turn to award-winning titles since the books have already been evaluated by a committee of professionals. Some teachers rely on these books so much that they fail to see how shifting societal sensibilities affect how readers and their parents respond to them. This is certainly true with *Julie of the Wolves* by Jean Craighead George (1973 Newbery Medal), first challenged for "sex and violence." Now, people question whether the Alaska Native people are presented accurately. Teachers must be prepared to discuss this point with their students. *Roll of Thunder, Hear My Cry* by Mildred D. Taylor (1977 Newbery Medal), set in the South during the Great Depression, deals with brutal racism. It is also a family story, and their effort to effect change in their Mississippi community. The controversy regarding Critical Race Theory (CRT) in school curriculum has caused challenges to this book. You cannot use Taylor's novel with students without discussing "the ugly side" of American history and applying the experiences of the Logan family to acts of racism today.

It's important to note that the intended audience for the Newbery Medal is birth to age fourteen. Titles like Cynthia Voigt's *Dicey's Song* (1983 Newbery Medal), Norma Fox Mazer's *After the Rain* (1988 Newbery Honor Book), Suzanne Fisher Staples' *Shabanu: Daughter of the Wind* (1990 Newbery Honor Book), and Avi's *Nothing But the Truth* (1992 Newbery Honor Book) are indeed intended for the upper age range. Elementary school teachers who buy entire Newbery collections for their third- and fourth-grade classrooms may wonder why their students aren't drawn to these titles. Forcing students to read these books when they aren't emotionally ready to deal with complex themes may turn them against reading and lead to potential challenges. If the young are granted the freedom to choose what they read, or if care is taken in selecting titles that do appeal to them at ages eight and nine, they will embrace those books for "older" readers later and have a positive reading experience.

Facing and Preventing Challenges

A sound and up-to-date collection development policy is the best defense in dealing with challenges to Newbery books or any materials in the library. School districts should have a similar policy for selecting novels taught in the Language Arts curriculum. Components to such policies include:

- The mission statement for the library and/or Language Arts curriculum
- The responsible parties for book selection
- Criteria for selection
- Statement regarding controversial materials
- Procedures for handling complaints

ALA OIF and the National Council of Teachers of English offer guidance and specific language in developing pertinent policies. It's easy to panic when someone challenges a book, but it's important to follow the policy and let the process work. Most book challenges don't result in an actual ban.

There are practical approaches to take in dealing with controversial books that may eliminate challenges from ever occurring:

- Communicate to colleagues, young readers, and their parents the literary elements that make a book "distinguished." Let them know that the Newbery Medal is chosen by a committee of professionals from all over the nation, who make their decision based on specific criteria for each pertinent genre. No consideration is given to whether a book might cause controversy.
- Know the books. It's difficult to effectively defend a title you don't know. At the very least, read the book when it has been challenged and before you enter a discussion with an angry parent.
- Recognize that it isn't the child's fault if a parent objects to a book. Quietly suggest a different title.
- Be prepared to offer an alternative title with similar themes to any student whose parent questions a book being taught in the classroom. A parent doesn't have the right to make curriculum decisions.

- Allow young readers to reject books that don't interest them. Most will reject what they aren't ready for.
- Read aloud a book exactly as the author has written it. Students may read along, or later read the book, and note omitted language or passages. This signals a nervousness about "problematic" issues and sends a message that censorship is okay.
- Address "problematic" parts in a book when children raise questions about the issues.
- Let go of old Newbery titles. Children shouldn't be asked to read all Newbery titles. Winning the Newbery Medal doesn't guarantee that a book becomes a classic, and out-of-touch stories don't serve the needs and interests of contemporary readers. Few students would have a desire to read *The Story of Mankind* by Hendrik Willem van Loon (1922 Newbery Medal). And, though *It's Like This, Cat* by Emily Cheney Neville (1964 Newbery Medal) was considered a groundbreaking book at the time, this novel wouldn't speak to children in the twenty-first century.
- Above all, plan open and honest discussion with young readers about an entire book. Explain why it's never appropriate to take words and scenes out of context. It's not fair to the book, to the writer, or even to readers. They must see the book as a whole if they are to learn how to properly respond to literature. This allows them to shape their own views regarding the compelling journey an award-winning book offers.

Getting Readers Involved

Here are examples of how to engage young readers in discussion about specific Newbery-winning titles that have language or scenes that could cause controversy:

- *Holes* by Louis Sachar (1999 Newbery Medal) has been challenged for "profanity." Discuss the setting of the book. Explain how Stanley Yelnats and each of the other guys wound up at Camp Green Lake. What does the language reveal about the culture of the camp? How does Stanley grow as a person during his time at the camp?

- *Kira-Kira* by Cynthia Kadohata (2005 Newbery Medal) has been challenged because of the prejudice that the Takeshima family endures. Cite the specific scenes of prejudice in the novel. Compare the prejudice they endure with the prejudice the Watson family faces in *The Watsons Go to Birmingham—1963* by Christopher Paul Curtis (1996 Newbery Honor Book). Both books are set in another era. How are incidents of cultural and racial prejudice today similar to what these two families suffered? Suggest ways to deal with prejudices and bigotry in your school and community.
- The science fiction novel *The House of the Scorpion* by Nancy Farmer (2003 Newbery Honor Book) has been challenged because of human cloning. How is cloning in conflict with the religious beliefs of some people? Discuss ways to explain the novel to those who are uncomfortable with the themes and topics in the novel. Explain how Matt, the clone of El Patrón, represents "good" and El Patrón stands for "evil." How does "good" win in the novel?
- *Wringer* by Jerry Spinelli (1998 Newbery Honor Book) is problematic to some because of incidents of bullying and violence. Identify the bullies in the novel. What is "the treatment"? How is this similar to initiation or hazing that occurs in clubs and fraternities? Contrast the way Palmer's mother and father react to "the treatment." Explain why Palmer refuses the initiation. What messages about bullying and violence does Spinelli relate to readers through Palmer?

Not everyone agrees about what makes a book "distinguished," but opinions should be solicited from the people who matter the most—the children. When a woman wrote an article for *Once Upon a Time*, a newsletter for children's writers and illustrators, that *Shiloh* wasn't appropriate for children, a group of sixth-graders sent letters to the editor and expressed their opinions about the book. She printed all their letters and stated that these students changed her mind. One girl wrote:

> Although this book consists of a terrible man named Judd Travers who abuses and kicks his dogs, curses, spits, and chews tobacco, it is proven in the book what a cruel man he is. I think that any child wouldn't want to be like this terrible man. I think Judd is an influence for children to grow up more like Marty, the loving main character.

This was a student who understood the meaning of Naylor's award-winning book. Distinguished literature is supposed to evoke an emotional response and cause young readers to ponder life—the good, the bad, and the ugly. Allowing children to read books as they are written opens their eyes to the world in which they live, and challenges them to contemplate the complexities of life. The writers of Newbery Medal and Honor Books open windows. It's up to professionals to pull back the curtains and allow children to see in.

Beyond the Book
ADDITIONAL RESOURCES/READINGS

Bobbitt, Randy. *Controversial Books in K-12 Classrooms and Libraries: Challenged, Censored, and Banned.* New York: Lexington, a division of Rowman and Littlefield, 2019.

Doyle, Robert P. *Banned Books: Defending Our Freedom to Read.* Chicago: American Library Association, Office for Intellectual Freedom, 2017.

Garnar, Martin, editor, and Trina Magi, assistant editor. *Intellectual Freedom Manual,* Tenth Edition. Chicago: American Library Association, Office for Intellectual Freedom, 2021.

Scales, Pat R. *Books under Fire: A Hit List of Banned and Challenged Children's Books,* Second Edition. Chicago: American Library Association, Office for Intellectual Freedom, 2021.

Scales, Pat R. *Teaching Banned Books: 32 Guides for Children and Teens,* Second Edition. Chicago: American Library Association, 2019.

Extending the Story

Activities to Enrich Newbery Reads

RAMONA CAPONEGRO, DENISE DÁVILA, ALPHA SELENE DELAP, AND LORA DEWALT

GROUP DISCUSSIONS AND OTHER LITERATURE-RELATED ACTIVITIES HELP children personally connect with books and characters, enriching their reading experience and engaging them in deeper thought. In this chapter, we present thirty-six Newbery titles with discussion prompts and ideas for further exploration.

This diverse collection of fiction, historical fiction, nonfiction, and poetry titles will provide numerous opportunities to involve young readers in spirited dialogue and meaningful activities.

Fiction

Because of Winn-Dixie by Kate DiCamillo
(Somerville, MA: Candlewick, 2000)
HONOR BOOK, 2001
A stray dog leads ten-year-old India Opal Buloni from one new friend to the next in a small Florida town. Stories she hears from each help her piece together a new definition of family.

Discussion Questions

1. Opal experiences a great deal of change in a short time. Who does she meet who helps her handle all the new aspects of her life?
2. If you were Opal, how would you describe what "home" means?

3. Through her conversations with characters—Miss Franny Block, Amanda Wilkinson, Otis, and Gloria Dump—Opal learns the universal nature of suffering. How does the idea that everyone has their own stories of sadness, fear, and anger affect your view of the world?

Activities

1. Opal's relationship with Winn-Dixie is very special. Have you had an animal in your life that has made you feel safe and known? What type of animal was it and did you give it a name? Reflect on the experiences that you had with your beloved animal friend and write a short thank-you note to this animal. Be sure to mention some of the most important experiences you had with it.
2. Home can be a place, a person, and/or an internal sense of safety, or a combination of all three. Use a box—shoebox size or smaller—to gather a few artifacts that symbolize where, with whom, and how you feel at home. Share these artifacts in a video and explain why you chose each artifact.

Bridge to Terabithia by Katherine Paterson, illus. by Donna Diamond (New York: Crowell, 1977)

MEDAL WINNER, 1978

Fifth-graders Jess and Leslie, a new girl, become friends, creating an imaginary world, Terabithia, in the woods. When tragedy strikes, Jess, shocked and despairing, slowly discovers the wonders Leslie left him.

Discussion Questions

1. Terabithia is one of the most important places to Jess and Leslie, and they hold some parts of Terabithia as sacred, only visiting there on special occasions. Jess also thinks of the art gallery he visits with Miss Edmunds as sacred, like Terabithia's pine grove. What's a place that's special or sacred to you, and what makes it so special?
2. Jess is afraid of many things, and he berates himself for his fears. What does he learn about fear from Leslie, Janice, May Belle, and other characters?
3. Jess and Leslie are teased and criticized for not fulfilling stereotypical gender roles. What do you think of expectations about there being

certain ways to behave like a girl or like a boy, and how would you respond to the characters who make these remarks?

Activities

1. Just as Leslie and Jess created Terabithia out of their imaginations, create your own Terabithia. You may choose to give your imagined place another name and a different setting, but design an imaginary place in which you could be your best self. Draw or write about this special place, how you would get there, and what you would do there.
2. After Leslie's death, Jess makes a funeral wreath for her and places it in Terabithia's sacred grove. Construct your own tribute for Leslie. It can be a wreath, a drawing, an obituary, a poem, or something else that would honor Leslie's life. In creating it, think about what Leslie means to Jess and what she means to you.
3. "Free to Be You and Me," written by Stephen Lawrence and Bruce Hart, is the song that the class is singing when Jess changes his mind and decides to become friends with Leslie. Listen to the song and consider why Paterson may have selected it for this moment in the story. Create a playlist of other songs that you think would fit well in the story and share why you selected these songs to accompany certain moments or events.

Crown: An Ode to the Fresh Cut by Derrick Barnes, illus. by Gordon C. James (Chicago: Bolden/Agate, 2017)

HONOR BOOK, 2018

In a vibrant, joyful tribute to the barbershop experience, a young Black boy relishes in the majesty of a fresh new haircut.

Discussion Questions

1. The narrator tells us getting a fresh cut is "the gold medal you." What is your "gold medal you" moment when you feel amazing?
2. What do you love the most about your current haircut/style? Were you nervous or excited before getting it done? Why or why not?
3. Why are barbershops and salons so important for a community? Why do you think they are often spaces of joy?

Activities

1. Draw yourself, a friend, or a family member with a fresh cut. Use the vivid colors and illustrations from Gordon C. James as inspiration. Then around your drawing add adjectives from *Crown* that feel true to you: royalty, intellectual, brilliant, blazing, important, etc.
2. Write a letter to someone who makes you feel like royalty, intellectual, brilliant, blazing, and/or important, etc. Use the words from Derrick Barnes as mentor sentences if you need help coming up with ideas for the content of your letter.
3. Think about being a barbershop or salon owner as a career. Research the process to become a barber or beauty professional in your state. What training is needed? What kind of license do they need? What are the biggest challenges and rewards? Use digital resources and interview someone in your community (or see if your school system has a cosmetology program).

Genesis Begins Again by Alicia D. Williams
(New York: Atheneum, 2019)

HONOR BOOK, 2020

Painfully self-conscious about her dark skin, thirteen-year-old Genesis faces new challenges when her family moves to suburban Detroit and she starts a new school.

Discussion Questions

1. Genesis finds strength and hope in music, inspired by the words, artistry, and resilience of Billie Holiday, Ella Fitzgerald, and Etta James, among many others. Which contemporary musicians can you think of who instill a similar sense of empowerment and love of self in the face of racism and sexism?
2. What artists, musicians, actors, and creative individuals motivate you? What qualities do they share? How are they different?
3. Why do you think that the main character's name is Genesis? And why does Genesis, which means the beginning, begin again?

Activities

1. Put together a playlist of songs from *Genesis Begins Again*. Share this playlist with others and learn more about the artists you have never

listened to before. Research one of the musical artists and put together a brief essay highlighting essential biographical details including a brief discography (list of hit songs).

2. Use a digital curation tool like Pinterest to gather images of beauty (your own subjective definition) from around the world. Use this Pinterest board to analyze your own sense of what makes a person beautiful. Discuss the board with your friends and peers and see if you can analyze similarities and differences. Challenge yourself to expand your sense of what is beautiful.

Hello, Universe by Erin Entrada Kelly (New York: Greenwillow, 2017)

MEDAL WINNER, 2018

In this story told from various viewpoints, including a bully, a deaf girl, a fortune-teller, and more, a rescue is performed, revealing bravery in the midst of fear.

Discussion Questions

1. Take a detailed look at the front cover. What do you notice now that you have finished the book? What connections to the story can be made right from the cover?
2. Erin Entrada Kelly has said the original title was going to be *Virgil and Valencia*. Do you think that is a good title or do you prefer *Hello, Universe*? Why do you think she changed the title to *Hello, Universe*? What other alternative titles do you think would be good for this book and why?
3. Which of the four main characters (Virgil/Turtle, Valencia, Kaori, Chet "The Bull") do you think changes the most throughout the story? Which character was your favorite and why? Which character was most like you and why?

Activities

1. This story is told from each character's point of view. Create a four-part adventure story with four "main characters." Think about what makes each person unique and their personal interests when crafting your story. Where does your adventure take you? What would you learn about one another along the way?

2. Pah, the large bird that frightens Virgil, is a part of the Philippine Mythology of Mindanao. Read the story as told by Mabel Cook Cole from The Project Gutenberg (www.gutenberg.org/files/12814/12814-h/12814-h .htm#d0e3634). Then, create a visual product (e.g., graphic organizer, Venn diagram) that compares the ways in which Pah is depicted in the original folktale and in the novel *Hello, Universe*. As an extension, investigate other folktales from the Philippines.

3. Erin Entrada Kelly said in her ALA Newbery Medal acceptance speech that her "greatest wish as a writer is that the person reading her book, or any book for that matter, feels less alone." Think about how the author and characters help make others feel less alone. Create a list as a class of things you can do to help people in the school feel less alone. What can be done individually? What can you do collectively as a group?

Last Stop on Market Street by Matt de la Peña, illus. by Christian Robinson (New York: Putnam, 2015)

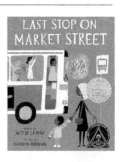

MEDAL WINNER, 2016

CJ's journey with his Nana is not just a bus ride; it is a multi-sensory experience through which he discovers that beautiful music, nature, and people surround him.

Discussion Questions

1. When CJ asks why a neighborhood is dirty, Nana says, "Sometimes when you're surrounded by dirt, CJ, you're a better witness for what's beautiful." What does Nana mean, and where can you see beauty in this book and in your surroundings?

2. Nana has an imaginative way of seeing the world. She sees a tree drinking through a straw and a bus breathing fire. What's something you see all the time, like a tree in the rain or a bus, that you can describe in a way that creates an action image?

3. The people CJ and Nana encounter are all part of a shared community. How do the characters help one another, and what are ways you can help people in your community?

Activities

1. Like the blind man, Nana, CJ, and the spotted dog on the bus, listen to a song with your eyes closed. How does the music make you feel? What do

you see inside yourself while you're listening? Listen to several kinds of music to see how various songs make you feel and envision different things.

2. Endpapers lead readers into and out of a story, and in this book, all of the items in the endpapers can be found in the illustrations. Search for the items in the endpapers in the interior illustrations and think about what the items add to the story. Design new endpapers for the book, thinking about other items from the words and illustrations you'd like to highlight or other ways you could lead readers into and out of the story. Looking at endpapers in other picture books may help you to get more ideas.

3. After you've read the book at least once, think about how beauty can be found through all five senses. Read the book again, looking or listening for words and phrases that appeal to the different senses. Take a walk through your school, library, or neighborhood, trying to observe with as many senses as possible. Share your observations through descriptive writing, as well as a drawing or collage.

Merci Suárez Changes Gears by Meg Medina (Somerville, MA: Candlewick, 2018)

MEDAL WINNER, 2019

Eleven-year-old Cuban American Merci Suárez balances the demands of her multi-generational family with the challenges of being a scholarship student at a private school in Florida.

Discussion Questions

1. In many communities, it is traditional for several generations of family members to live together. In the United States, elderly people often live in what are called "senior living homes" where they can receive professional care and medical support. Which would you prefer, to live with your family or in a senior living home when you are elderly? Why?

2. What does Merci's experience of her grandfather's memory loss teach her?

Activities

1. Build a "memory place" of five aspects of your life that are important to you right now. Find five artifacts that reflect who you are and what you

care about. Create a mini encyclopedia of these five artifacts, providing a definition of what they are, how you use them, and what they mean to you.

2. To release stress, Merci rides her bike. Research the bike trails and paths in your town, city, or neighborhood. Create a bike map with these trails and paths that is accessible on the internet using geographical/topographical software such as Google Maps.

New Kid by Jerry Craft (New York: HarperCollins, 2019)
MEDAL WINNER, 2020

A funny, thought-provoking graphic novel that details Jordan Banks' seventh-grade year as one of the few African American kids in an elite suburban school.

Discussion Questions

1. Jordan experiences a range of micro aggressions.
   What is one of them, and how does he represent it in comic form?
2. Jordan feels like he must be a "chameleon" to fit into his home neighborhood and his new private school. What is one way he must change himself to fit in?

Activities

1. The main character, Jordan, uses art, specifically cartooning, to express his hopes and fears. Divide a piece of paper into six squares. Write down three of your own fears and three hopes—one per square. Draw an image that represents each emotional experience, hope, or fear. Pick one of the images you feel open to sharing and explain the drawing through the completion of the prompts: 1) What is the emotional experience you are trying to represent? 2) Do you remember a recent time when you felt this experience strongly? What happened? 3) How does what you drew connect to your experience?
2. Jordan is the "new kid" at school. Describe a time when you were a "new kid" to a place, an experience, or a person. The "new kid" experience doesn't have to be in a school context; you could be the new kid visiting another place or trying a new hobby or extracurricular activity. It could be when you made a new friend. Write a short six-word memoir related

to this "new kid" experience. Now take the memoir and find digital images, using an internet search engine, to represent each word in your memoir. Create a slide show to share with others.

Other Words for Home by Jasmine Warga
(New York: HarperCollins/Balzer & Bray, 2019)
HONOR BOOK, 2020

Themes of conflict, home, identity, the arts, and prejudice are interwoven in this powerful verse novel about a Syrian girl's new life in America.

Discussion Questions

1. In *Other Words for Home*, food is synonymous with home. What foods represent home to you? What smells and tastes remind you of your family and close friends? Is there one food that reminds you of being a young child?
2. "Middle Eastern" is a new cultural concept for Jude, the main character. Can you imagine why this attribution might be confusing and feel imprecise and even problematic?

Activities

1. Create a collage of images and words that represent your favorite foods, ingredients, tastes, and smells. Use the website Food Timeline (www .foodtimeline.org) to research the first documented use of each of the ingredients in your collage. Add chronological labels to each item.
2. Using Wikimedia Commons (commons.wikimedia.org), search for "Syrian food," create a presentation of images that include a range of dishes and beverages important to Syria. Label the dishes and beverages mentioned by Jude in *Other Words for Home*.

Show Way by Jacqueline Woodson, illus. by Hudson Talbott (New York: Putnam, 2005)

HONOR BOOK, 2006

Jacqueline Woodson's poem *Show Way* tells the story of slavery, emancipation, and triumph for each generation of her maternal ancestors—the women who guided their daughters to courage, self-sufficiency, and freedom.

Discussion Questions

1. Why do you think it was so important for Mathis May (Soonie's grandma) and her great-grandmother to each take a piece of their family blanket with them when they were enslaved and stolen from their families?
2. Woodson doesn't give Soonie's mama a name. Instead she writes "a girl-child who was born free that same year, 1863. History went and lost her name. . . ." Why do you think the author chose to include that sentence? How does it make you feel as a reader? Why is it important to remember people even if their names are lost to history?
3. The author tells us that each child was "loved up" even if they were living in harmful situations (enslaved or segregated). How do you see the children loved in the words and illustrations of this book? What do the people in your life do to "love up" on you both in joyful times and times that are really difficult?

Activities

1. Create a family tree of the characters in *Show Way*. Use a timeline to show the family history from Soonie's great-grandmother all the way to Toshi. Include the family traits that traveled from generation to generation across their family tree.
2. Quilts provided directions to escape enslavement as brave people ran from those who tried to hold them captive. As a class, take a virtual tour of the National Quilt Museum (quiltmuseum.org) or the Smithsonian Institution National Quilt Collection (www.si.edu/spotlight/national -quilt-collection). Which quilts are similar to those in the illustrations by Hudson Talbott? Which quilts are your favorite from the illustrations and the museum? Why? Draw or create your own quilts in response to *Show Way*.

***The Tale of Despereaux: Being the Story of a Mouse, a Princess, Some
Soup, and a Spool of Thread*** by Kate DiCamillo, illus.
by Timothy Basil Ering (Somerville, MA: Candlewick,
2003)

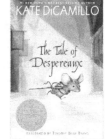

MEDAL WINNER, 2004

Despereaux, a smaller than usual mouse in love with music,
stories, and a princess named Pea, undertakes a hero's quest
that culminates in mice, rats, and humans living almost
happily ever after.

Discussion Questions

1. The narrator tells us that love, hope, and forgiveness are powerful,
   wonderful, and ridiculous. How do love, hope, and forgiveness fulfill
   these descriptors in the story, and how have you seen them be powerful,
   wonderful, and ridiculous in other situations?
2. Which rules are broken in the mice, rat, and human communities, and
   what do the consequences reveal about the characters and the rules?
3. After the death of the queen, soup brings the king great sadness, but
   soup brings comfort to Cook and Despereaux. What is something that can
   make you feel sad, comforted, or both, and why does this item make you
   feel this way?

Activities

1. The book's narrator has a distinctive voice and often goes beyond telling
   the story by asking questions of the readers and providing observations
   about the events and characters. In the coda at the end of the book, the
   narrator asks to be thought of "as a mouse telling you a story." Draw a
   picture of how you see the narrator and write a description of the
   narrator's personality, based on how the narrator speaks to you while
   telling the story.
2. Despereaux is the title character, and the book's subtitle describes
   elements of the story that are especially relevant to him. As befitting
   the title character, he is also on the book's cover. However, Chiaroscuro,
   Miggery Sow, and Princess Pea are also main characters. Select one
   of these characters and name the story after them, such as *The Tale of
   Miggery Sow*. Create a subtitle for the tale, highlighting aspects of the

story that are important to the character you chose, and design a book cover featuring that character.

3. Darkness and light are often compared in the story. Using black and white scratchboard, create an image of light entering darkness and what it might reveal. You can purchase black and white scratchboards or readily find techniques online for creating your own.

Where the Mountain Meets the Moon by Grace Lin (New York: Little, Brown, 2009)

HONOR BOOK, 2010

A rich tapestry of stories, both original and traditional, transports readers to a fantastic world where Dragon joins Minli on a fortune-changing quest.

Discussion Questions

1. Minli, the main character, hears many stories at home and on her journey. In some stories, characters try to change their fates and fortunes, like the goldfish man, Magistrate Tiger, and Wu-Kang, and their efforts are met with mixed results. Other characters, like Da-A-Fu's ancestors, accept their fates or like A-Fu and Da-Fu, do not wish to change their fortunes. How does Minli's idea about changing her family's fortune shift during the story, and what do you think are the benefits and consequences of seeking change or accepting what you have?

2. Minli has amazing adventures, though she is lonesome, frightened, and even in danger at times. Ma and Ba decide to return home without Minli, and they are sad and afraid as they wait for her return. What fortifies Minli and her parents while they are apart, and is it harder to go on an adventure or to wait for an adventurer to return?

3. The Old Man of the Moon only answers one question from one visitor every ninety-nine years. What question would you ask the Old Man of the Moon?

Activities

1. Lin credits Chinese folktales with inspiring her stories. Read some Chinese folktales and see what connections you can find between the folktales and the stories in Lin's book. Consider how the folktales may

have inspired elements of Lin's stories and illustrations. The "Behind the Story" section in the paperback edition provides some specific character sources.

2. The Old Man of the Moon connects people with red threads. Create a character web that shows how different characters are connected to one another. Create another web that shows how you are connected to other people. Find a way to include the color red in your webs.

3. Some of Minli's adventures and the stories shared with her are accompanied by illustrations that depict specific moments. Look at these illustrations and think about the events from the stories that they highlight. Select one of your favorite stories from the book and create an illustration that depicts an important event within that story.

Historical Fiction

Elijah of Buxton by Christopher Paul Curtis (New York: Scholastic, 2007)

HONOR BOOK, 2008

Elijah is the first free-born child in Buxton, a Canadian community of escaped slaves, in 1860. With masterful storytelling, humor, and insight, Curtis takes readers on a journey that transforms a "fragile" boy into a courageous hero.

Discussion Questions

1. Why do you think it's important to read about historical events, such as when enslaved people were escaping to freedom? How can we learn about real events from fictional characters like Elijah?

2. How much of the book do you think reflects people's experience in the world today? Even though it's historical, what is still the same? Where can you find commonalities with your life and the lives of Elijah, Ma and Pa Freeman, the Preacher, Cooter, Emma, Mr. Leroy, Mrs. Holton, and Mrs. Chloe?

3. Which part of the story surprised you the most as a reader?

Activities

1. Research Frederick Douglass. What can you learn about his life that Christopher Paul Curtis included in *Elijah of Buxton*? Present your research in the form of a speech or booklet.
2. Elijah is brave because he put himself at risk traveling to the United States. Write about a time you were brave and did the right thing (even if it was hard). What did you do? How did you feel? What was the outcome? How did other people respond?
3. Create a visual timeline of each chapter in *Elijah of Buxton*. For each chapter choose two to three sentences that stand out as important and include those quotes in your visual representation. You can create your timeline by hand or use digital tools.

Inside Out and Back Again by Thanhha Lai (New York: HarperCollins, 2011)

HONOR BOOK, 2012

Hà and her family flee war-torn Vietnam for the American South. In spare yet vivid verse, she chronicles her year-long struggle to find her place in a new and shifting world.

Discussion Questions

1. Which poem was your favorite? What drew you to that poem? Why was that poem important to Hà's story? Is there a particular line or lines in the poem that you think are especially well written?
2. How is Hà similar to other characters we have read about in class? Which other fictional characters do you think she would be friends with if book characters from different stories could meet?
3. Hà has a difficult time when she immigrates to the United States as a refugee. She struggles with the language, culture, food, and people at school (plus wondering about her father back in Saigon). What can we learn from Hà's experience about being a refugee?

Activities

1. Poems are meant to be savored aloud. With a small group, choose one to two poems from the story and practice reading them aloud. Practice which words you want to emphasize with volume, which words you want

to speak slowly, and any words that are new to you. You do not need to memorize them (unless you want to!). Then share a poetry slam with the class, taking turns reading poems from the novel out loud.

2. As a class, find out what local resources support refugees near you. Call or email them to see how you can help. What supports do they need? They might need physical resources, or they might need support for students who are joining your school—like a guide for newcomer students. What can you do to help other kids like Hà who are new to the United States? If you have emigrated from another country, what do you wish you had when you first arrived at school?

Kira-Kira by Cynthia Kadohata
(New York: Atheneum, 2004)
MEDAL WINNER, 2005

This nuanced novel glitters with plain, poignant words that describe the strong love within a Japanese American family from the point of view of younger sister Katie. Personal challenges and family tragedy are set against the oppressive social climate of the South during the 1950s and early 1960s.

Discussion Questions

1. How is the connection to Japanese culture expressed?
2. What does *kira-kira* mean? How does the concept manifest throughout the story in different ways?
3. Why is it important that the novel is situated in the American South in the 1950s?

Activities

1. Katie Takeshima lives within two cultures simultaneously. Imagine if Katie had a social media account. How would she represent herself in words and images on this account? Put together Katie's mock account emphasizing distinct aspects of her Japanese American experience.
2. The book's cover has Katie and her sister Lynn in the middle of a Georgian field. With a cell phone camera, recreate this cover wearing items representing your own cultural heritage in a landscape (outside) that is

part of your everyday life: a parking lot, a mall, etc. Share this photo in a brief slideshow detailing the differences between your photo and the *Kira-Kira* cover. Explain the specific choices you made when recreating the photo and how your own heritage is expressed.

The Night Diary by Veera Hiranandani
(New York: Kokila/Penguin, 2018)

HONOR BOOK, 2019

Told in the form of diary entries addressed to Nisha's dead mother, this novel traces a mixed-faith family's flight from Mirpur Khas, Pakistan, to Jodhpur, India, during the partitioning of India in 1947.

Discussion Questions

1. What do you know about the history of the India-Pakistan partition? Why and how did it come about?
2. Imagine the region you live in divided up and many of your friends and family living in another country even though they never moved. How would you feel?
3. Why is it important that Nisha's twin brother, Amil, is given an illustrated book of tales from the *Mahabharata*?

Activities

1. Create a timeline of the India-Pakistan partition during the time of India's independence from British rule. Include images that symbolize how people must have felt.
2. Research the Bengal and Punjab provinces and create a recipe book of dishes and ingredients that were important to the people of these areas. Make sure to explore the four different types of dishes: charbya, chosya, lehya, and peya. Include images of ingredients and dishes.
3. Draft a series of diary entries written by Nisha's twin brother, Amil. Imagine that Amil is writing about his experience five years after the partition as his family prepares to move to the United States. He is now a teenager and thinking about the changes in his life and his future life.

One Crazy Summer by Rita Williams-Garcia
(New York: HarperCollins/Amistad: 2010)

HONOR BOOK, 2011

Set in 1968 Oakland, California, three sisters find adventure when they are sent to meet their estranged poet-mother Cecile, who prints flyers for the Black Panthers.

Discussion Questions

1. The main characters, Delphine and her sisters Vonetta and Fern, have certain expectations of their estranged mother before they visit her in Oakland for the summer. How does Cecile differ from how they thought she would be? How is Cecile different from how you have been taught to think about mothers in general?
2. The Black Panther Party supported their community in a range of ways. What were those ways and why were they important? Do you see some of these same programs in existence today?

Activities

1. In the United States, mothers are expected to be certain ways, and popular culture constructs stereotypes of motherhood: self-sacrificing, ever patient, eager to please and entertain, and nurturing. Who are some maternal characters from books, television, and movies who fit with these stereotypes? Can you think of maternal characters like Cecile in *One Crazy Summer* who defy the dominant expectations?
2. Research a group or organization that was inspired by the Black Panther Party. Create a paper or digital poster highlighting the ways in which the organization has used the goals of the Black Panther Party to work toward social and economic justice in the twenty-first century.

Roll of Thunder, Hear My Cry by Mildred D. Taylor (New York: Dial, 1976)

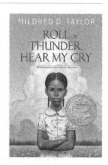

MEDAL WINNER, 1977

The vivid story of an African American family whose warm ties to one another and their land give them strength to defy rural southern racism during the Depression.

Discussion Questions

1. The Logan family and other members of their community stand up against racism, using a variety of approaches to respond to injustice. What do different characters risk by standing against racism, and why do they continue to work toward equity?
2. Their family's land is very important to the Logans. Why are they determined to hold onto it, and why is Mr. Granger determined to take it away?
3. T.J. Avery repeatedly makes poor choices regarding his schoolwork, his friends, and his future, yet the Logans, the Averys, Mr. Morrison, and Mr. Jamison strive to protect him as much as they can. What motivates T.J.'s decisions, and what motivates the other characters to protect him?

Activities

1. A book's front cover is intended to reflect the spirit of the book and entice people to read it. Since this book was published, multiple artists have created covers for it. Check your library or search the internet for different covers and consider which covers best capture the book's characters, plot, setting, and themes. With these elements in mind, design your own cover for the book and explain how it relates to the story and encourages people to read the book.
2. The Logans are one of the few African American families in their community to own land. Most of the other African American families are sharecroppers. To understand more fully the lives of the Averys, Turners, and other families in the book, research sharecropping in the United States after the Civil War. Create a poster that explains how sharecropping operated and its effects on people's lives. Include examples from your research and Taylor's book on your poster.
3. Although this book is set in the 1930s, its central concerns about addressing racism and creating a more just society are still relevant today. After

discussing the ways in which members of the Logan family and other members of their community respond to racism, access some "antiracism for kids" resources online and strategize ways in which you can help to make your school, library, and community antiracist and inclusive.

A Single Shard by Linda Sue Park
(New York: Clarion, 2001)

MEDAL WINNER, 2002

In twelfth-century Korea, Tree-ear, an orphan fascinated with a community of potters, begins assisting Min, the master potter. When Min entrusts Tree-ear with precious artwork to be delivered across unknown territory, the orphan must rely on his courage and wits to prove himself worthy of Min's trust.

Discussion Questions

1. What character traits does Tree-ear show throughout the book? How do those traits help him to be successful?
2. What are the major themes in *A Single Shard*? Although the book is set a long time ago, do you think the themes are still relevant today? Why or why not?
3. The details of the pottery are so important to the story and show the characters as artists. How is pottery still important in our lives today? Why do you think so many pieces of pottery are in museums? Do you believe pottery is an art that will stand the test of time in our future? Why or why not?

Activities

1. *A Single Shard* has had a few different covers since it was originally published. Look up images of the different covers. Which do you think best depicts the story of Tree-ear? If you could redesign the cover, what would you include? How could you re-imagine the book cover to hook additional readers? Create a new cover either by hand or using digital tools.
2. Create a booktalk/sales pitch to persuade other readers to pick up *A Single Shard*. Include your favorite part of the story, information about the

themes of the text, and some of the awards it won, including the New-bery Medal. Also, leave some suspense for the future reader. Record your booktalk/sales pitch and share it with the class.

The Watsons Go to Birmingham—1963 by Christopher Paul Curtis (New York: Delacorte, 1995)
HONOR BOOK, 1996

From hilarious opening chapters to a shattering conclusion, this novel, narrated by fourth-grader Kenny Watson, brings to life an African American family in Flint, Michigan, in 1963. The depiction of devastating events in Birmingham integrates the dichotomy of familial love and stability with the racial strife of the 1960s.

Discussion Questions

1. Kenny spends a lot of time thinking about his big brother, Byron, and trying to understand his actions and motivations. What do you think of Byron, and how does your opinion of him change throughout the story?
2. Kenny sees the Wool Pooh when he is caught in the whirlpool and looking for Joetta at the church. What or who do you think the Wool Pooh is, and what do you think of Kenny's and Byron's different ideas about the Wool Pooh?
3. The book has fifteen chapters. How does the story change in the last three chapters, and how do the first twelve chapters contribute to the ending?

Activities

1. Kenny repeatedly refers to his family as the "Weird Watsons," especially when they're acting in ways he finds funny or embarrassing. Think about whether his family seems that weird or unusual to you and which of Kenny's stories about his family you most enjoyed. Write a story about a time you found your family or another group funny or embarrassing.
2. The book is told from Kenny's perspective. How might one of the stories be different if it were told by Byron, Joetta, or another character? Select one of the stories Kenny tells about his family or school and retell the story from another character's perspective, reflecting on how two characters may see the same event differently.

3. The Watsons don't discuss the civil rights movement until they begin planning their trip to Birmingham, and Curtis shares more specific historical details in the front and back matter of the book than in the story itself. Read some nonfiction works, including picture books, about the civil rights movement. Larry Dane Brimner's *Birmingham Sunday* and Carole Boston Weatherford's *Birmingham, 1963* provide especially relevant historical context to the church bombing the Watsons experience. After reading at least one nonfiction work about the civil rights movement, compare the information you find in the books and write a short essay explaining why you think Curtis may have decided to write about the bombing from Kenny's fictional perspective.

The Wednesday Wars by Gary D. Schmidt (New York: Clarion, 2007)

HONOR BOOK, 2008

Seventh-grader Holling Hoodhood is convinced his teacher hates him. Through their Wednesday Shakespeare sessions, she helps him cope with events both wildly funny and deadly serious.

Discussion Questions

1. When Holling thinks his teacher, Mrs. Baker, hates him, his sister tells him to get some guts. What does she mean, and how do you see different characters getting guts throughout the book?
2. Holling wants to be able to make choices about his own future and worries that he won't get the opportunity. Which characters do you think decide who they want to become and take steps toward these envisioned futures, and what do you think prevents other characters from doing so?
3. Mrs. Baker tells Holling that Shakespeare wrote "to express something about what it means to be a human being." What ideas about being human are expressed by Shakespeare and Schmidt, and how would you tell or show someone what it means to be human?

Activities

1. During the 1967–68 school year, the Hoodhoods watched Walter Cronkite deliver the nightly news. Select one of the historical events or figures included in the story, such as the Vietnam War, Martin Luther King Jr., or

Bobby Kennedy, and write a news report about this event or person. To get some more ideas about events during this time, you may want to read the nonfiction collection *1968: Today's Authors Explore a Year of Rebellion, Revolution, and Change*, edited by Marc Aronson and Susan Campbell Bartoletti.

2. As he reads Shakespeare's plays, Holling relates ideas and events from the plays to things happening in his life. Select one of your favorite stories from a book, play, movie, TV show, video game, or other medium and relate that story to an event in your life, perhaps through a similar theme, character, or plot twist. You may also choose to apply an aspect of one of your favorite stories to an event in Holling's life.

3. Play scripts follow certain conventions as they introduce characters and settings and provide stage directions, monologues, and dialogues. Look at a play by Shakespeare or another playwright to observe these conventions. Then adapt a scene from the book into a script format, so the scene can be performed.

Wolf Hollow by Lauren Wolk (New York: Dutton, 2016)
HONOR BOOK, 2017

In this coming-of-age story, spunky and courageous Annabelle defends a veteran who has become the target of local bullying attacks.

Discussion Questions

1. Why was World War I called both the "Great War" and the "war to end all wars"?

2. What is bullying? Why do you think that Betty bullies other people? What do you think would be the best ways to stop bullying? How is Betty like the fascist leaders of World War II?

3. Imagine how Wolf Hollow, Pennsylvania, is different or similar to where you live. How do you think the place you live now has changed since 1943?

Activities

1. Toby is a veteran of World War I. Research the specific ways that World War I was different than other wars before it. Write a letter to Toby with

questions about his experience during and after the war. Include your understanding of the unique circumstances of World War I. Now, imagine that Toby writes you back. What do you think he would write? Write a response that extends and adds to the information you have learned about Toby in the book.

2. Create an advertisement, paper or digital, against bullying. Provide a definition of bullying and evidence of its negative effects. Make sure to include a powerful image that relates to your definition directly. Write a voice-over script and record yourself explaining the ad in PowerPoint or FlipGrid.

3. The one-room schoolhouse is central to *Wolf Hollow*. Use the Google image search engine to locate images of one-room schoolhouses in the 1940s in the United States. Once you have examined the photographs and, in particular, the students' desks, draw two desks, one from a 1940s schoolhouse and one from your own school classroom.

History/Nonfiction/Biography

All Thirteen: The Incredible Cave Rescue of the Thai Boys' Soccer Team by Christina Soontornvat (Somerville, MA: Candlewick, 2020)
HONOR BOOK, 2021

With superb narrative nonfiction writing, Soontornvat skillfully describes the dramatic real-life rescue of the Thai Boys' soccer team in 2018.

Discussion Questions

1. Soontornvat describes ways in which caves, such as Tham Luang, can be both intimidating and inviting. After finishing the book, how do you see caves as more frightening and more amazing, and what other things can be both dangerous and wonderous?

2. Multiple teams and leaders were part of the rescue mission. What teams were involved in the rescue, and how did the team members work together? Who were some of the leaders, and what traits of leadership did they show?

Activities

1. Watch some of the recorded news coverage and/or read some of the articles written about the rescue. Soontornvat's bibliography provides some sources, and others are easily found on the internet. Consider which figures and aspects of the rescue are featured or excluded from the news stories and why journalists may have made these choices. Create your own account of the rescue, addressing the entire mission or focusing on specific events or people. These accounts can be presented as written articles, video broadcasts, or oral presentations.

2. Coach Ek and the Wild Boars meditated before their soccer games and in the cave in order to stay focused and calm. Read Soontornvat's introduction to meditation and try at least one meditation exercise from a book or website. Reflect on how you feel after completing the meditation once or regularly over a period of time and make a list of situations in which meditation might help you, just as it helped Coach Ek and the boys.

3. Soontornvat included multiple explanations and diagrams about the science of cave formation, the flooding conditions in Tham Luang, and the divers' route through the cave's chambers. In order to understand more fully the conditions in which the rescue mission occurred, perform some of the condition simulations that Soontornvat describes, such as wetting a sponge to saturation and oversaturation, instigating an acidic reaction by putting limestone in vinegar, creating different levels of water pressure with a hose, and examining sumps within pipes. Other activities related to the formation of caves, stalactites, and stalagmites can be found in science experiment books and on websites.

An American Plague: The True and Terrifying Story of the Yellow Fever Epidemic of 1793 by Jim Murphy (New York: Clarion, 2003)

HONOR BOOK, 2004

Drawing from primary sources, such as private diaries, newspapers, and books, Murphy gives insight into the multifaceted challenges of the yellow fever epidemic. The compelling narrative engages readers, illuminates the community's responses, and shows the best and worst of humanity.

Discussion Questions

1. What are the differences and similarities between the yellow fever epidemic in the eighteenth century and the twenty-first century's COVID-19 pandemic?
2. Think about the communities of first responders during both public health emergencies. What supports did they provide, and how did they provide support? What were the differences and similarities between them?
3. How does Allen and Jones' pamphlet, *A Narrative of the Proceedings of the Black People, During the Late Awful Calamity in Philadelphia, in the Year 1793*, mirror the critical analyses of the twenty-first century Black Lives Matter movement and contemporary instances of institutional racism?

Activities

1. The Free African Society evolved into the AME (African Methodist Episcopal church), which has been instrumental in American movements for social justice and civil rights. Research the AME using three different expert reference sources. Create an interactive timeline of AME contributions around the United States; make sure to include images and music along with historical detail including complete attributions.
2. Beginning with *An American Plague*, create a scrapbook of yellow fever newspaper clippings, illustrations, and cartoons. Next, using web-based image search engines, add in newspaper clippings, illustrations, cartoons, and memes about COVID-19. What similarities and differences do you see?
3. Create a new book cover for *An American Plague* using Canva or another graphic design platform. Incorporate digitized images that highlight the contributions of free Black people in Philadelphia during the late eighteenth and early nineteenth centuries.

Bomb: The Race to Build—and Steal—The World's Most Dangerous Weapon by Steve Sheinkin (New York: Roaring Brook/Flash Point, 2012)

HONOR BOOK, 2013

A riveting thriller told in three parallel stories: the race against time to build the world's first atomic bomb; the determination to stop the Nazis from developing it first; and the stealthy efforts of Soviet spies to steal the American plans.

Discussion Questions

1. In Sheinkin's *Bomb*, there are three countries at the center of the story. How is each of these countries engaged in the development of nuclear weapons during the 1940s?
2. Photographs are a very important part of the book. Which photographs were the most interesting to you and why?
3. What were the environmental effects of nuclear testing at the Bikini Atoll near the Marshall Islands after World War II?

Activities

1. Using Google Earth, create a map of the different geographical areas of the world discussed in *Bomb*. Try to be as specific as possible. Label the areas with historical details that you excavate from the book. Do your best to map out the football stadium in Chicago, Illinois, the laboratories in eastern Tennessee, the high desert location of Los Alamos in New Mexico, and the other locations critical to the history.
2. Research the life of German chemist Otto Hahn. Use at least three different biographical sources to create a presentation that highlights his various discoveries and the circumstances in which he was awarded the Nobel Prize.
3. Examine environmental effects of nuclear testing on the Bikini Atoll, including recent work by Stanford University in 2017. Create a poster of images of the tests and the results of these twenty-three tests over fourteen years.

BOX: Henry Brown Mails Himself to Freedom
by Carole Boston Weatherford, illus. by Michele Wood (Somerville, MA: Candlewick, 2020)
HONOR BOOK, 2021

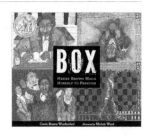

The true story of Henry "Box" Brown, who shipped himself to freedom in a box, is told in fifty-one emotionally intense poems that have implications for the present day.

Discussion Questions

1. Henry's escape cannot happen independently. He must rely on others too. How is community important in this story? What can we learn as members of a community about helping others?
2. Each poem is composed of a title and a six-line stanza. Why do you think the author, Carole Boston Weatherford, chose that structure to tell the story of Henry Brown? What do you notice about the use of punctuation throughout the poems? How does that impact us as readers?
3. Read the illustrator's note, and then talk about what you think the illustrator wants readers to know about Henry Brown based on their tone and imagery. Why do you think they included a variety of colors and textures and backgrounds collaged throughout the story?

Activities

1. Primary sources are used throughout the story of *BOX: Henry Brown Mails Himself to Freedom.* Use resources such as the Library of Congress and Henry Brown's *Narrative of the Life of Henry Box Brown: Written by Himself* to identify and view additional primary resources. What else can you learn about Henry Brown through these images and words?
2. Create a list of interview questions you would want to ask Henry Brown if he were alive today. What would you want to know about his life before, during, and after his journey to freedom? What questions could you ask him that would help his story to be told for future generations?
3. Select another famous historical person to research. Perhaps it is another formerly enslaved person or perhaps it is another individual who exemplifies bravery and love. Once you have done some research, write a poem, of six lines, sharing what you learned about that person's life. Be sure to include a title.

Brown Girl Dreaming by Jacqueline Woodson
(New York: Penguin/Nancy Paulsen, 2014)

HONOR BOOK, 2015

In a lyrical memoir, Woodson's elegant stand-alone poems weave a story about her development from a struggling reader and dreamer into a confident young woman and writer.

Discussion Questions

1. Woodson has published works of poetry and prose. Why do you think she chose to write her memoir as a collection of poems, and what connections do you see between her free verse form and her focus on memories?

2. Family and place are very much connected for Woodson: the Woodsons in Ohio, the Irbys in South Carolina, and her immediate family in Brooklyn. What are some similarities in how she writes about the various people and places, and how are certain people connected to certain places for you?

3. Woodson recalls significant events in her life, her family, and the United States, such as the civil rights movement. She also writes about everyday things that were important to her, such as books ("stevie and me," "the selfish giant"), songs ("music"), games ("another way," "game over"), and treats ("the candy lady"). What are some of the everyday things that are most important to you, and what do you want to remember about them?

Activities

1. Ten "how to listen" haiku are interspersed among the other poems. Read these ten haiku together. Why are they in a different form than the other poems? How do the haiku and their shared idea of listening encapsulate different aspects of Woodson's story? Write your own "how to" haiku or series of haiku, focusing on an important element of your personal story. Arrange your haiku in a visual collage with Woodson's haiku.

2. Woodson provides different models of activism by mentioning well-known people, such as Martin Luther King Jr., Malcolm X, James Baldwin, Rosa Parks, Ruby Bridges, and Angela Davis, as well as different approaches to activism people have taken: nonviolent resistance, marching, writing, and caring for the marchers. Research various activists and

ways to take action and create a guide of different ways people can change the world.

3. One of the final poems, "What I Believe," lists many of the things Woodson believes in, things that she has written about throughout the book. Create your own list poem, declaring various things in which you believe.

El Deafo by Cece Bell, illus. by the author (New York: Amulet, 2014)

HONOR BOOK, 2015

In an insightful and humorous graphic novel memoir, Bell portrays growing up with a giant hearing aid strapped to her chest. Themes of navigating a new school, finding a true friend, and a first crush make this book universal in appeal.

Discussion Questions

1. Cece Bell said she "felt like a superhero." What are the greatest strengths of El Deafo? What are your superpowers?
2. Which visuals in this graphic novel biography helped you learn the most about Bell's life?
3. What do you think the author believes about friendship?

Activities

1. Create a fictional magazine based on the interests, attributes, and personality of El Deafo. Include a name for the magazine and a short description of what the magazine offers its readers. Write one to two articles for the magazine about a topic of interest for the character. Include other items found in magazines too, such as an advice column, recipes, advertisements, infographics, and anything you believe the character would enjoy reading. Consider using print and digital magazines as mentor texts.
2. Imagine you are hired to introduce this book to new readers as part of the publishing team. What would be the book's slogan? What questions would you ask the author in an interview? What type of readers would be interested (*If you loved _____, you'll also love* El Deafo!) and/or what signage would a library or bookstore need to entice someone to pick up the text?

Create a marketing plan, including a digital booktalk or trailer, to grow the audience of *El Deafo*.

3. Cece Bell tells the story of her childhood in *El Deafo* and won numerous awards for her writing. Explore her website, social media accounts, and videos of her interviews. Consider the following in your author study: What did you learn about Bell as a writer? What did you learn about her as an individual? What surprised you most after exploring her digital presence? What would you ask her if you ever got to meet her?

Freedom over Me: Eleven Slaves, Their Lives and Dreams Brought to Life by Ashley Bryan, illus. by the author (New York: Atheneum, 2016)
HONOR BOOK, 2017

In the United States, slaves were erroneously considered objects with a monetary value. Here, Bryan humanizes eleven enslaved people, imagining the dreams and personal reflections that belong only to them.

Discussion Questions

1. Some people believed humans could have a price, but this book shows what is priceless about the human spirit, our dreams, and our experiences. What did you notice about how the eleven people in this story played, celebrated, and contributed to their community? How can we continue to honor them in our work, play, and celebrations?

2. The book's words and images show contrast between dreams and reality, both for the people who were enslaved and for the people who enslaved them. How does the impact of slavery continue to impact both our dreams and our realities today?

3. What do you see in the art of Ashley Bryan? Why do you think he chose to include real documents, collages, and bright backgrounds for the pages?

Activities

1. *Freedom over Me* is unique because it was a Newbery Honor Book and a Coretta Scott King Honor Book. Use the American Library Association website to review the criteria for Newbery winners and Coretta Scott

King Book winners. Compare and contrast the awards. What other titles can you find that were honored by both prestigious award committees?

2. As a class, read reviews of *Freedom over Me*. Talk about what makes a strong book review—what components does that genre of writing usually include? As a class, write a review together for *Freedom over Me*. Then in pairs or individually, write reviews for other books by Ashley Bryan or Newbery winners/honors.

3. Even though Ashley Bryan's book is historical, human trafficking is still a problem today across the world. This book shows us the importance of not putting a price on people's lives. The US State Department's website has resources for how you can help fight human trafficking. The Department of Homeland Security's Blue Campaign has a guide entitled *How to Talk to Youth about Human Trafficking* (www.dhs.gov/sites/default/files/publications/blue_campaign_youth_guide_508_1.pdf) that can be used to teach students modern-day examples, warning signs, online safety, and more. Partner with your school counselors, social workers, and administrators to support student safety.

Hitler Youth: Growing Up in Hitler's Shadow by Susan Campbell Bartoletti (New York: Scholastic, 2005)

HONOR BOOK, 2006

Weaving the personal stories of twelve young Germans into the larger fabric of Nazism and World War II, Bartoletti elevates understanding of Hitler's strategic plans of manipulation to a new level.

Discussion Questions

1. At the height of the Hitler Youth movement, the organization had more than seven million young members. Why did so many children and teenagers join the movement enthusiastically, why did others join reluctantly, and why did some resist?

2. Adolf Hitler relied on Germany's youth to prepare and carry out the war effort. How did being members of the Hitler Youth give young people power, and, at the same time, take power from them?

3. During World War II, reports and rumors spread in Germany about the atrocities taking place in the concentration camps. After the war, the

Allies used documentary films about the death camps to educate young people and adults. Why do you think many Germans, including members of the Hitler Youth, were so reluctant to accept that the stories about the concentration camps were true?

Activities

1. The book focuses on the experiences of Hitler Youth members and young people who resisted the Nazis, but millions of other people lost their lives or had their lives forever changed during World War II. Read some picture books, historical novels, and other nonfiction works about World War II and the Holocaust to learn more about the war's global reach and the impacts it had on different communities, particularly Jews and others who were persecuted by the Nazis.
2. Helmuth Hübener, Karl-Heinz Schnibbe, Rudi Wobbe, Hans Scholl, Sophie Scholl, and Christoph Probst resisted the Nazis by distributing information about the government's agenda and activities. Other young people, as well as adults, also resisted the Nazis. Research different stories of Nazi resistance. You can also research the stories of young activists today. Create a chart showing what these activists have in common, as well as the different ways they undertake their work.
3. The book includes photographs of Hitler Youth members, as well as Nazi resisters. Select a photograph that stands out and examine it closely. What may the photograph reveal about a person? Write an interior monologue for the photographed person, capturing what they might be thinking and feeling in that moment.

The Voice That Challenged a Nation:
Marian Anderson and the Struggle for Equal Rights
by Russell Freedman (New York: Clarion, 2004)

HONOR BOOK, 2005

Eloquent prose sheds a personal light on one woman's sometimes reluctant role as a symbol in the struggle against racism and her calling to share an illustrious gift.

Discussion Questions

1. What did you already know about Marian Anderson and/or segregation in the arts prior to reading this book? What information did you learn?

What information surprised you? What information confirmed or validated something you already knew?

2. What characteristics do you see in young Marian Anderson that carried through her life? Why do you think Russell Freedman included details about Marian's entire life rather than just focusing on her experiences with civil rights as an adult?

Activities

1. PBS' *American Experience* has a great recording available on YouTube of Marian Anderson singing at the Lincoln Memorial. Create a video in response about how it makes you feel to hear her voice come to life and what you admire about Marian Anderson after reading her biography.

2. Russell Freedman explains that Eleanor Roosevelt supported Marian Anderson by publicly resigning her Daughters of the American Revolution membership when Marian was not allowed to perform at Constitution Hall. Use the American National Archives (www.archives.gov/exhibits/american_originals/eleanor.html) to read Mrs. Roosevelt's letter. Then write a persuasive letter standing up for an issue of equity in your community.

3. Consider the text features that are included in *The Voice That Challenged a Nation*. Create a T-Chart that lists each text feature and how it helped you as a reader to develop a stronger understanding of the story that Freedman was creating.

Poetry

Carver: A Life in Poems by Marilyn Nelson
(Asheville, NC: Front Street, 2001)
HONOR BOOK, 2002

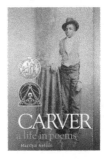

Told from multiple perspectives, this collection of poems reveals little-known facts about the remarkable scientist George Washington Carver. Nelson transcends Carver's brilliance and achievements to present the essence of this profoundly humble man.

Discussion Questions

1. Did the titles of any of the poems surprise you? Which title do you think is a very strong fit? What in the poem works well with that title?

2. Which poem confused you the most? What do you think Nelson was trying to describe in that poem? What words can we use to simplify the most confusing part?

3. What patterns do you see across a few poems? Are there words, ideas, or themes that keep coming up in multiple poems? What do you think that pattern tells us as readers?

Activities

1. Select one poem from the biography and look up news events from that year (and location if noted), using the Library of Congress Chronicling America website (https://chroniclingamerica.loc.gov). (For example, after reading "Prayer of the Ivory-Handled Knife," a student could search from 1871-72 the word "ivory-handled knife" and find an article from the *Nashville Union and American* offering a knife as a prize for the best boiled ham.) What do you notice about the news during the time of George Washington Carver's life? Create a class timeline of news events alongside events from the text.

2. Find an article on George Washington Carver to read after finishing *Carver*. Highlight or circle important words in the article, then create a "found poem" that can be paralleled to the poetry presented by Nelson.

3. Create a modern-day model of one of the poems using physical items to represent that poem. Include at least one item that represents the theme of the poem. For example, you might select an alarm clock, a text message chain, and a coffee mug to represent the early morning communication and commitment to working long hours in "Veil Raisers."

The Crossover by Kwame Alexander
(New York: Houghton Mifflin Harcourt, 2014)

MEDAL WINNER, 2015

Twelve-year-old narrator Josh uses the rhythms of a poetry jam to emulate the "moving and grooving/popping and rocking" of life on the basketball court. This novel paints an authentic portrait of a closely knit family on the brink of crisis.

Discussion Questions

1. Do you think that *The Crossover* would have been just as enjoyable if it had been written in traditional prose (i.e., not verse)? Why or why not?
2. Which character inspires you the most? How so?
3. What significance does the theme of "crossing over" play in the story?

Activities

1. Think about a sport or physical activity you enjoy. Write down the sounds, smells, and textures you experience when you are playing or taking part in that favorite physical activity. Write a series of four haikus, with five (line 1), seven (line 2), and five (line 3) syllables. Make sure to include a sound, a smell, and a texture in each haiku.
2. Imagine you were going to write a screenplay to turn *The Crossover* into a movie. How would you map out the opening scene? What music would be playing? What elements would the camera focus on? What would the light be like? What set of feelings would you try to convey?

Joyful Noise: Poems for Two Voices by Paul Fleischman, illus. by Eric Beddows (New York: Harper, 1988)

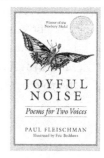

MEDAL WINNER, 1989

Fourteen poems offer a look at what insects might think of themselves and their world. Soft yet often comical black-and-white pencil drawings accompany the poetry.

Discussion Questions

1. The poems have different rhythms, structures, and tones. How does each poem reflect the featured insect's activities?

2. The poems vary by featuring insects as individual bugs (the moth and digger wasp), as pairs or small groups (the book lice and cicadas), and as a collective (the whirligig beetles and house crickets). Despite this variety, why do you think all of the poems were written for two voices?

3. Based on the accounts of the insects' lives featured in the poems, which insect would you most want to be and why?

Activities

1. The note at the beginning of the book explains how the poems were written to be read aloud. Find a partner, and following Fleischman's instructions, prepare to read one of the poems together. It will probably take you multiple tries to find the poem's rhythm and the timing and delivery you want. Reflect on how the poem becomes more meaningful as you practice and your performance improves. Consider how you experience the poem differently when you read it aloud with a partner and when you read it silently on your own. If you have enough people, you can stage a reading of various poems in the book or the whole collection.

2. The illustrations vary in how realistic they are and the extent to which human characteristics have been given to the insects, a process called anthropomorphization. Compare photographs of the various insects with the illustrations of those insects. How much have they been anthropomorphized in the illustrations? Draw two new versions of a featured insect, one that is as realistic as possible and one that adds more human characteristics and accessories to the insect, making sure these additions are associated with the insect's thoughts and actions in the poem.

3. Each poem provides some basic information about an insect, as well as a descriptive or fictionalized account of the insect's behavior. Research an insect from one of the poems to learn more about its life cycle and activities and create a nonfiction entry about the insect to accompany the poem.

Out of the Dust by Karen Hesse
(New York: Scholastic, 1997)
MEDAL WINNER, 1998

Fourteen-year-old Billie Jo learns to cope with her mother's death and her grieving, withdrawn father in a story of survival, courage, and love set in Depression-era Oklahoma.

Discussion Questions

1. Billie Jo and her father suffer difficult losses. How do they grieve their losses differently, and how do they find their way back to each other?
2. Like many other characters, Billie Jo tries to get "out of the dust" by leaving. However, she quickly changes her mind and returns home. What causes her to leave and return, and what factors do you think most contributed to people's decisions to seek new opportunities or to remain where they were during the Dust Bowl?
3. In "Thanksgiving List," Billie Jo notes "the certainty of home, the one I live in / and the one / that lives in me." What do you think she means when she talks about home this way, and how do you envision home as a place or a feeling?

Activities

1. The Dust Bowl is an event with both natural and human causes in a specific geographic area. Research the different causes and look for examples of how Hesse incorporated them into the story. You can also look at online photographs of the dust storms in the western United States in the 1930s and compare them with Hesse's descriptions of the storms and their aftermath.
2. Hesse portrays one family's life in the Dust Bowl through free verse poems. Matt Phelan's graphic novel, *The Storm in the Barn*, offers another fictional perspective on the Dust Bowl, whereas Don Brown provides a graphic nonfiction account in *The Great American Dust Bowl*. Read at least one of these graphic works and compare how the Dust Bowl is presented in this work and in Hesse's book. Think about the contents of the books, as well as their mediums.
3. Billie Jo describes contemporary events that intrigue her or intersect with her life, such as President Roosevelt's birthday ball, the birth of the Dionne quintuplets, the eruption of Kīlauea, and Prohibition. Consider a

current event that you find interesting or that connects with your life in some way. Write a free verse poem about the event and your interest or connection to it.

The Surrender Tree: Poems of Cuba's Struggle for Freedom by Margarita Engle (New York: Holt, 2008)
HONOR BOOK, 2009

Free verse in alternating voices tells the story of Cuba's three wars for independence from Spain. At the center is Rosa, a traditional healer, who nurses those in need.

Discussion Questions

1. What did you learn about Cuba from reading this novel in verse? How does that compare to what you know about history in the United States? In other countries?
2. How did Engle connect each poem to create the five parts? What structures did you notice in each of the five parts? What patterns did you notice across the five parts?
3. There is a lot of nature imagery and vocabulary throughout the book. Why do you think the author made the decision to connect a story of a country's wars with the beauty of the natural world?

Activities

1. Work with a small group to bring the novel-in-verse to life. Act out two to three of the poems and take on the role of the characters such as Rosa and Silvia. If needed, add dialogue to the poems to help the audience follow your re-creation of the story.
2. As a class, take a virtual field trip to Cuba using digital resources (e.g., Nearpod: www.nearpod.com, Virtual Field Trips: www.virtualfieldtrips .org). Keep a travel log of what you notice about the country on your remote travels. What questions do you want to explore if you ever have the chance to visit Cuba yourself?
3. Rosa is based on a nurse who healed soldiers from both sides of the wars, Rosario Castellanos or Rosa la Bayamesa. Lt. Death and Lt.-Gen. Valeriano Wegler are based on soldiers. Write to a medical professional or military member and tell them about this book. Create a list of questions you have about their careers based on the experiences of characters in the text.

Beyond the Book

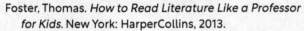
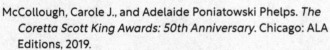

ADDITIONAL RESOURCES/READINGS

Foster, Thomas. *How to Read Literature Like a Professor for Kids*. New York: HarperCollins, 2013.

McCollough, Carole J., and Adelaide Poniatowski Phelps. *The Coretta Scott King Awards: 50th Anniversary*. Chicago: ALA Editions, 2019.

Mlawer, Teresa, and Nathalie Beullens-Maoui, eds. *The Pura Belpré Award 1996–2016: 20 Years of Outstanding Latino Children's Literature*. New York: Rosen, 2016.

Prose, Francine. *Reading Like a Writer: A Guide for People Who Love Books and for Those Who Want to Write Them*. New York: HarperCollins, 2006.

Front and Center

Ideas for Promoting Your Newbery Book Collection

KIMBERLY PROBERT GRAD

SINCE ITS BEGINNING IN 1922, OVER FOUR HUNDRED BOOKS HAVE RECEIVED a Newbery Medal or Honor, and chances are your library holds many of these titles. But how can you make the most of your Newbery collection? This chapter explores ways to promote Newbery Award-winning and Honor Books in public and school libraries, through mock book discussions and elections, programming, booklists, and book displays. The goal is to bring visibility and awareness of these titles and the award itself to young readers with an emphasis on promoting reading for fun and creating opportunities for literacy gains.

Mock Book Discussions and Elections

Mock Newbery discussions and elections can be richly rewarding experiences for the hosts and attendees. Through these programs, participants, both children and adults, can gain a better understanding of and appreciation for the Newbery Award and its winners. And, at the same time, readers also are introduced to newly published books and can develop the skills to evaluate children's literature with a critical point of view that goes beyond likes and dislikes. Mock Newbery programs can be as simple (a one-time event) or as complex (a yearlong process) as desired and can be centered on young readers, adults, or both. To simulate the experience of the actual Newbery Award selection process, books should be evaluated and voted on according to the guidelines for the actual award. The goal is to select the most distinguished title published for children in the year preceding the award.

ALSC offers two comprehensive resources, *Guide to Planning a Mock Newbery Discussion and Election* and *Newbery and Caldecott Mock Elections Tool Kit*, which provide guidance for hosting mock discussions and elections. The aim of this chapter is to share some highlights, tips, and program ideas from the field to help inspire you.

Timing Is Everything

The process and timeline for Mock Newbery discussions and elections (or Newbery book clubs as they are called in some schools) are typically based on the timing of the Newbery Award committee's selection process, thereby harnessing some of the excitement of the real-life Newbery experience. While the actual committee is in its suggestion-and-nomination phase during the fall months, mock book groups can begin the process of selecting their titles, ordering multiple copies of these books, and scheduling their discussion meetings from October to December, building up to a final discussion prior to ALA's Youth Media Awards announcements in late January or early February.

Engaging Book Discussion

The success of Mock Newbery programs depends greatly on quality dialogue among participants. The *Guide to Planning a Mock Newbery Discussion and Election* recommends having participants practice summarizing main points and comparing and contrasting books to get them comfortable and prepared for the discussion ahead. To encourage the expression of diverse opinions, the guide suggests asking readers to think about how their own backgrounds and biases might affect their thought processes while reading. It's important to encourage participants to keep an open mind as they read about new experiences and concepts that are unfamiliar to them.

The Cooperative Children's Book Center (CCBC) Book Discussion Guidelines are a trusted resource in planning for book discussions. Developed by Ginny Moore Kruse and Kathleen T. Horning, Cooperative Children's Book Center, University of Wisconsin-Madison, the guidelines are widely accepted as best practice for ensuring effective, pithy book discussion. The straightforward strategies in the guide help steer discussion away from the sharing of simple story summaries and digressions into personal experiences. The key is to keep conversation focused on the books, starting with positive comments and then moving into concerns or difficulties. Additional tips in the CCBC guidelines are designed to create an environment where there are no "wrong" answers and where all feel welcome to share their unique perspectives, which can lead to more robust discourse. (For the URL for the guidelines, see the resource list at the end of this chapter.)

Most important for a Newbery book discussion is to first review the criteria used by the actual award selection committee in their evaluation of titles. In *Guide to Planning a Mock Newbery Discussion and Election*, criteria from the *Newbery Award Committee Manual* are presented with interpretive questions that get the conversation started and moving in the right direction.

- **Interpretation of theme or concept:** Is there a sense that the author's essential messages are being conveyed successfully through characterization, plot, style, and setting?
- **Presentation of information including accuracy, clarity, and organization:** If you are reading historical fiction, biography, or nonfiction, are the historical details accurate? If you are reading science fiction, do you notice a solid base in scientific fact?
- **Development of plot:** What is happening in the story? Is there a distinguishable story arc and is it memorable?
- **Delineation of characters:** Has the author provided a believable approach to characters with appropriate dialogue and development?
- **Delineation of setting:** Do you have a sense of the world in which the story takes place? How well is the setting developed? How does the setting enhance or complement the story?
- **Appropriateness of style:** Does the text flow? Are the vocabulary and sentence structure appropriate? Is it written in the first or third person? How does the style contribute to the story?
- **Presentation for a child audience:** Would a young reader consider the book to be readable? Do you get a sense that the author is "showing" facts rather than "telling"?
- **Illustrations** should only be considered if they distract from the text.[1]

Ideas from the Field: Newbery Book Clubs at School

Kim Sigle, an elementary library specialist in Fairfax County Public Schools in Virginia, hosted a Newbery Book Club with fifth- and sixth-grade students at the Lake Ann Elementary School in Reston, Virginia. Over the course of several weeks, the students learned about the award and talked briefly about Newbery Medal-winning and Honor Books that they had read. They played a Newbery trivia game and discussed the difference between a book that is distinguished and worthy of the Newbery Award versus a book that is popular and fun to read. They discussed the criteria for the award, focusing on plot, theme, characters, setting, and style. And they read stacks of newly published books.

Sigle's students had the opportunity to summarize a book after they had finished reading it and to share their thoughts on why it should or shouldn't be considered for the award. They used graphic organizers to note their thoughts on each book. And the CCBC Book Discussion Guidelines were used as the starting point for their discussions. Weekly booktalks generated interest in the books that were well received.

In setting up her student discussion group, Sigle was inspired by a video produced by colleague Susie Isaac, who has hosted student-based mock elections for eight years as a teacher and librarian in the Cherry Creek School District in Colorado and was a member of the Newbery 2022 selection committee. In Isaac's video, which promotes and celebrates mock discussions and elections, her students express their delight in the experience, saying that "Newbery Club made me want to read a lot more," Newbery Club was a "life changer for me," and "Reading is going to be the new thing to do—the cool thing for once."

For her mock programs, Isaac created discussion prompts, based on the Newbery criteria, to specifically address one aspect at a time, creating manageable discussions for each session. A "mirrors and windows" prompt aided readers in discussing whether or not they saw a reflection of themselves in a book and what they might learn from the reading experience. Isaac also utilized an overall feedback form to help students gather their thoughts. Additional content included a prompt for coaching students on how to defend their choice, with questions such as "What is so distinguished about your favorite book? Why were the characters so believable and real to you? What was so powerful about the author's message? Why does this book matter?" After all, as one student remarked in the video, "Nobody in this whole club has the same opinion." The full list of Isaac's discussion prompts is included in *Guide to*

Planning a Mock Newbery Discussion and Election (see URL in the Note at the end of this chapter).

Mock Newbery elections typically culminate in an exciting voting process. This can be especially engaging when the group follows some or all of the ballot procedures used by the actual Newbery committee.

Susan Polos, librarian at Greenwich Country Day School in Greenwich, Connecticut, found that in setting up her Newbery groups, it was helpful when scoring the results of the mock election to create a simple scoring sheet for the students to easily record their remarks and to keep their thoughts organized. Readers chose first, second, and third choices, much like the actual ballots. In order to take first place, a book had to receive a majority vote. Honors were chosen by how close the votes were to the winner. Balloting is covered in detail in *Guide to Planning a Mock Newbery Discussion and Election*.

To add even more excitement to her mock programs, Polos also created a banquet celebration, modeled after the actual Newbery/Caldecott/Legacy banquet, that took place several months after the voting process toward the end of the school year. This allowed for plenty of time to arrange virtual visits with the winning authors. The library was set up like a banquet hall with tablecloths, place settings, and a specially designed card featuring the winning covers on one side and the names of the mock committee on the other. Students dressed up and, sometimes, food or drink choices were matched to the winning titles. Children volunteered to announce the winners and to prepare the questions for the visiting authors.

Sigle also enhanced her book discussion experience by inviting two distinguished guest speakers to club meetings. One speaker was a local author who had won the Newbery, and the second was a librarian who had served on the Newbery Award Selection Committee. Not every mock program organizer is able to line up visiting authors. If that isn't a possibility, another option is to share the acceptance speeches given by Newbery-winning authors at the annual Newbery/Caldecott/Legacy banquet (see the URL in the resource list at the end of this chapter).

More Mock Opportunities

Mock discussions and elections also provide an opportunity for school and public library partnerships. Scheduling regular book club discussions during the school day or in an afterschool program could lead to one culminating event where the winners are chosen at the public library.

Many libraries hold mock discussions for staff members as a professional development exercise. At Brooklyn Public Library (BPL), the annual Mock Newbery discussion has often been described as one of the favorite professional development events of the year for children's librarians. The long-standing tradition of offering professional development to children's librarians at BPL was originally organized by Clara Whitehill Hunt, the library's first superintendent of Work for Children, who also conferred the first Newbery Medal to Hendrik Willem van Loon for *The Story of Mankind* in 1922.

The annual discussions at BPL are championed by the Library's Youth and Family Services department. A selection committee meets during the fall to choose about five or six titles that have the potential to lead to meaningful discussion on award criteria. Once the titles are selected and announced, librarians have a few weeks to catch up on their reading through late fall. Each year before ALA's Youth Media Awards are announced, the group of BPL children's librarians gathers on a wintery night for about two hours. It's a relatively short amount of time for such an engaging discussion, but it gives busy children's librarians a chance to discuss books with their colleagues and to spend valuable time together.

Liv Hanson at the Chicago Public Library organizes annual staff mock Newbery discussions and recently made the switch to a virtual platform using Zoom. Hanson found that Zoom's breakout room feature helped to manage the number of attendees and create smaller, more productive discussion groups. And virtual events can result in greater participation.

Whether a mock election program is for adults or children, part of the fun is sharing your group's results with other readers and Newbery enthusiasts. Each year, the ALSC Blog makes a call for mock election results and posts the mock winners of various ALA awards, including Caldecott, Newbery, Coretta Scott King, Geisel, Printz, Sibert, Pura Belpré, and Batchelder. It's an informative resource for finding out what young readers and librarian colleagues throughout the country are reading and recommending.

Programming around Newbery

As covered in the previous chapter, engaging, book-related activities can enhance the reading experience and reinforce comprehension. Activities utilizing art (redesigning the cover of a favorite Newbery book), writing prompts (writing a letter to your favorite Newbery character), and games (Newbery trivia) can be worked into the book discussion process or function on their own as library programs for children.

Social media can also be tied into Newbery-related programming, adding to the fun and raising awareness of your library's activities and Newbery collection. Join the community of book lovers on Instagram and add to sixty-six million #bookstagram posts with your group's book selections and winners. The best virtual book displays show carefully arranged books with thoughtful props, background setting, art, and use of color. Document your book group's progress each week on an account dedicated to your program. Take it one step further and invite your participants to produce a short TikTok or BookTok video to recommend their favorite Newbery titles from current or past years. Tie these projects into your school or library's overall social media approach by cross tagging on other platforms.

Developing Booklists

Think about the body of Newbery titles as a whole and consider the various ways these books can be sorted into reading lists that grab the attention of different audiences. These lists can also be used as the foundation for book clubs or displays. For example, compile titles by potential appeal to students in a particular grade, or by genre (historical fiction, science fiction, or fantasy), or by theme (stories about dogs, families, or journeys). Share your favorite lists on your library website, on bookmarks, or in displays. The following sample lists may spark your creativity and inspire you to build your own lists to kindle the curiosity of young readers.

Sample Booklists

GRADE: FIFTH
- *Brown Girl Dreaming*, by Jacqueline Woodson
- *The Crossover*, by Kwame Alexander
- *Echo*, by Pam Muñoz Ryan
- *The Girl Who Drank the Moon*, by Kelly Barnhill
- *The House of the Scorpion*, by Nancy Farmer
- *Merci Suárez Changes Gears*, by Meg Medina
- *One Crazy Summer*, by Rita Williams-Garcia

- *Roller Girl*, by Victoria Jamieson
- *The War That Saved My Life*, by Kimberly Brubaker Bradley
- *A Wrinkle in Time*, by Madeleine L'Engle

THEME: BOOKS WITH DOGS
- *Along Came a Dog*, by Meindert DeJong
- *Because of Winn-Dixie*, by Kate DiCamillo
- *Dogsong*, by Gary Paulsen
- *Ginger Pye*, by Eleanor Estes
- *The Inquisitor's Tale: Or, The Three Magical Children and Their Holy Dog*, by Adam Gidwitz
- *Shiloh*, by Phyllis Reynolds Naylor
- *The Underneath*, by Kathi Appelt

GENRE: HISTORICAL FICTION
- *Bud, Not Buddy*, by Christopher Paul Curtis
- *Crispin: The Cross of Lead*, by Avi
- *Criss Cross*, by Lynne Rae Perkins
- *Dead End in Norvelt*, by Jack Gantos
- *The Door in the Wall*, by Marguerite de Angeli
- *Dragon's Gate*, by Laurence Yep
- *The Evolution of Calpurnia Tate*, by Jacqueline Kelly
- *Kira-Kira*, by Cynthia Kadohata
- *The Midwife's Apprentice*, by Karen Cushman
- *Out of the Dust*, by Karen Hesse
- *Roll of Thunder, Hear My Cry*, by Mildred D. Taylor
- *The Witch of Blackbird Pond*, by Elizabeth George Speare
- *A Year Down Yonder*, by Richard Peck

GENRE: SCIENCE FICTION AND FANTASY
- *Doll Bones*, by Holly Black
- *The Girl Who Drank the Moon*, by Kelly Barnhill
- *The Giver*, by Lois Lowry
- *The Graveyard Book*, by Neil Gaiman
- *The Hero and the Crown*, by Robin McKinley
- *The High King*, by Lloyd Alexander
- *Mrs. Frisby and the Rats of NIMH*, by Robert C. O'Brien

- *The Tale of Despereaux,* by Kate DiCamillo
- *When You Reach Me,* by Rebecca Stead
- *A Wrinkle in Time,* by Madeleine L'Engle

Building Book Displays

After assembling booklists, the titles can be pulled from the collection to use in year-round book displays, supplementing the content with other similar titles. Consider additional purchases to round out the collection. If your library has a policy for labeling, think about purchasing or producing Newbery-themed spine labels. In addition, gold Newbery Medal or silver Honor seals are available at the ALA store for placing on book covers. Ask staff members for help in decorating displays with art, objects, and signage for extra appeal. Remember to keep the signage fresh and replace all worn-out elements when necessary.

Creating give-away items as your budget and schedule allow also can enhance visibility of the collection.

- Add bookmarks to books.
- Create shelf talkers for book displays.
- Produce T-shirts for book club discussion groups to create a sense of reading community and identity.

The most important thing to remember in working with your Newbery collection, whether it's with displays, lists, programming, or mock award discussions and elections, is to have fun and to promote the love of reading. Enjoy the process that you create based on the guidelines and tips shared here and customize for your purposes.

Acknowledgments

Thank you to the Newbery 100th Anniversary Celebration Task Force. Members include Susan H. Polos (Chair), Greenwich Country Day School, Greenwich, CT; Tom Bober, School District of Clayton, MO; Kimberly Probert Grad, Abbot Public Library, Marblehead, MA; Sawako Shirota, Candlewick Press, Somerville, MA; Kim Christiansen Sigle, Fairfax County Public Schools, VA; Catherine Elizabeth Sorensen, Scarsdale Schools, NY; and Jordan Dubin, ALSC staff liaison.

Beyond the Book

ADDITIONAL RESOURCES/READINGS

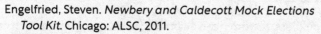

"Book and Media Awards Shelf." ALSC, 2021. https://alsc-awards-shelf.org/.

Engelfried, Steven. *Newbery and Caldecott Mock Elections Tool Kit.* Chicago: ALSC, 2011.

Kruse, Ginny Moore, and Kathleen T. Horning. "CCBC Book Discussion Guidelines, 1989." Cooperative Children's Book Center, School of Education, University of Wisconsin-Madison, last modified 2021. https://ccbc.education.wisc.edu/literature-resources/ccbc-book-discussions/ccbc-book-discussion-guidelines/.

"Newbery Medal Seals (Gold)." ALA Store. www.alastore.ala.org/content/newbery-medal-seals-gold.

"Past Newbery, Caldecott and Legacy Banquet Acceptance Speeches." ALSC, 2021. www.ala.org/alsc/awardsgrants/bookmedia/NCWBanquetRecordings.

NOTE

1. *Guide to Planning a Mock Newbery Discussion and Election,* Newbery 100th Anniversary Celebration Task Force, 2021, www.ala.org/alsc/mock-newbery-toolkit.

Putting the Newbery to Work

Advocating for Youth Services Library Workers

CASSIE CHENOWETH

PICTURE THIS: YOU'RE MEETING FRIENDS FOR COFFEE ON A SUNNY SATUR-day afternoon. Because your friends know you work in a library, the topic of favorite books comes up. A friend mentions *The Westing Game* by Ellen Raskin, a childhood favorite of the group. Everyone jumps to talk about their experience reading the classic. You mention in passing that it is one of your favorite Newbery winners. The group looks at you with realization; they remember the gold sticker on the front of their school library's copy. They haven't thought about the Newbery in years (they're not watching the Youth Media Awards [YMAs] livestream on January mornings like we do)! This is your time to shine. This is the time to tell your friends about all the recent Newbery winners and honors that, even as adults, they would love. You tell them about *New Kid* by Jerry Craft, *Hello, Universe* by Erin Entrada Kelly, and *Brown Girl Dreaming* by Jacqueline Woodson and how easy it is to pick up one at their local library. When the conversation moves on to other topics, you realize you are an advocate.

What is advocacy? Advocacy is the public support of a cause. For our purposes, advocacy is the public support of youth services library workers and the services they provide.

As a well-known and respected hallmark of the profession of library service to children, the Newbery Award can be a powerful tool for raising awareness of the expertise and work of library workers serving youth and of the wealth of resources available at the library. Before we jump into advocacy, let's look at stakeholders and elevator speeches.

A Few Words about Stakeholders

Our primary stakeholders, as library workers serving youth, are the groups and individuals whom we reach directly with our resources, programs, and services, such as children, families, daycare centers, and schools. In this chapter, we focus on secondary stakeholders. These are members of the community who don't necessarily benefit directly from your library's programs and services, but they do share your commitment to supporting children and families. It's often necessary to actively seek out these colleagues. By developing relationships with these secondary stakeholders, we can build a wider base of support in the community. This chapter includes ideas for elevator speeches and activities that can be used to engage secondary stakeholders, including library management, trustees, and boards; government agencies; local media outlets; and your community.

What Is an Elevator Speech?

Elevator speeches are brief opportunities—a minute or less—to grab the attention of those you want to inform on the value of libraries and the work you do. When you have compelling elevator speeches in your tool belt, you're ready to take advantage of advocacy opportunities whenever and wherever they present themselves—at your library, the farmers' market, a community leader's office, or, yes, on an elevator.

The goal of your elevator speeches isn't to enumerate to your listener everything you do at the library. Instead, your speeches should focus on what you do and why your work is important. Successful elevator speeches prompt listeners to ask questions and request more information.

Value-based, action-oriented elevator speeches emphasize specific things you do and how they positively impact the youth and families you serve.

The elevator speeches provided below have the added twist of focusing on the Newbery Award to key in on that expertise of library workers serving youth and the value of the library's collection.

Now we're ready to jump in and explore some ways to put the Newbery Award to work in advocating for youth services library workers and the library. I hope these examples spark your creativity and provide a jumping-off point for future advocacy planning at your library.

Advocating to Library Management, Boards, and Trustees

Elevator speech: The winner of the Newbery Award was announced this morning. I can't wait to put together a display of the winner and honor books from years past. Did you know youth services workers like me chose the winners? I love how one of the more prestigious awards for children's literature comes from the most knowledgeable group.

Activity: Celebrate the Newbery announcements (cupcakes, sparkling grape juice, or maybe even a treat that ties into one of the winning books) with fellow library staff on the Monday of the announcements. It's your time to shine again. This is an opportunity for a little fun and staff camaraderie, and it highlights the children's services department and staff.

Activity: Share the winners at your next board/trustee meeting along with statistics on Newbery book circulation in your library. Demonstrate how this award chosen by youth services workers, among others, is valued by children, parents, publishers, and other professionals alike.[1] Highlight how these winning books are a valuable part of the library's collection. See the "Programming around Newbery" section in chapter 5 for some concrete ideas on how to demonstrate the value of the award and your collection through art, writing projects, social media posts, and more.

Advocating to Government Agencies

Elevator speech: I love helping kids and families find good books. Whenever I'm stumped, I look up a list of Newbery Award winners and Honor Books. Did you know that the Newbery has been around for one hundred years? It's chosen each year by youth services library workers like me. Your support helps the library stay on top of all the best books for kids.

Activity: Poll your young patrons, library staff, and board members about their favorite Newbery books now (or for adults—when they were growing up). Collect stories that demonstrate children's/adult's love for these books. How have these award books inspired and supported children's literacy and kindled a lifelong love of books and reading? Share these stories at opportune times, like when the year's winners are announced in January.

Activity: If your library hosts Newbery mock discussions and elections (see chapter 5), be sure to share results widely with library/school staff, management, parents, the community, and local politicians. Convey to these stakeholders that this fun and engaging activity hosted by the library helps young readers develop skills in discussing and evaluating children's literature and supports them in becoming engaged readers and thinkers.

Advocating to Local Media

Elevator speech: Have you received ALA's press release announcing the Newbery and other media award winners? Children's librarians are among the experts who choose the winners. I'm passionate about children's literature and finding the right book for each child at the library. I know that the right book in the right hands can ignite a child's love for reading and lifelong learning.

Activity: ALA's annual announcement of the Newbery and other book and media award winners could be an appealing hook for a local news outlet. Reach out to them with details about the Newbery, the new winners, and what your library offers in the way of distinguished children's books. It could lead to a news story about the library and its collection. Taking the time to initiate and cultivate positive relationships with the reporters who cover your library as part of their "beat" can be time well spent. As influencers of public opinion, reporters have a strong voice in your community, so it's important to get to know them.

Activity: If your library has hosted a Mock Newbery election, announce the winners in a press release to local media. Be sure to list the winning book and honor titles and what the children loved most about these titles. Include how many enthusiastic readers participated in the program and who at the library facilitated the discussion and election. Close the release with a statement that mock Newbery groups are inspired by the John Newbery Medal, which has been awarded annually since 1922 by the American Library Association to the most distinguished book for children.

Advocating to the Community

Elevator speech: Have you ever noticed the shiny stickers on some children's books? That means they've won an award for being among the best books of the year. One of the awards is called the Newbery Award. It's been around for one hundred years! And did you know it's chosen by youth services workers like me? So, you know it's going to be good. We have lots of winners and honor books available at the library for you to check out. Can I help you find some?

Activity: Share the year's newly minted winners on your social media channels. Let patrons know which of these distinguished titles are available at your library. Your library collection is a valuable asset for the community. Flaunt it!

Activity: Every year as spring arrives many communities open a farmers' market. Families fill the market supporting local businesses and farms. What about supporting their local library as well? Does your library have a booth at the market? A community event is the perfect time to advocate for your library and youth services. And what better way to attract kids and families to your booth than with a display of books with shiny gold and silver stickers on them? And you can change it up each week with a diverse selection of Newbery books to pique visitors' curiosity. In chapter 5, we share sample booklists by genre, theme, etc., which could inspire your booth display choices, too. Taking it one step further, consider offering storytime or poetry readings at the market that showcase Newbery titles. Be sure to let families know that the library offers children's and young adult books that have won many different awards and appeal to numerous audiences.

Activity: ALSC shares reaction videos created by winning authors in the weeks after the Newbery Award announcements. These videos are often entertaining, heartwarming, and funny, and sometimes include a big thank you to libraries and youth services library workers. Take the opportunity to share these videos on your social media accounts. Let patrons know which books by the author you have at your library.

Our Biggest Little Advocates

While this chapter has focused mainly on secondary stakeholders, I can't conclude without just a few words about our littlest, yet biggest, advocates—children. As mentioned earlier in this chapter, be sure to check out chapter 5 to learn ways that young people can use social media, such as Instagram and Tik-Tok/BookTok, in fun ways to share their favorite Newbery books, while at the same time spotlighting your library and collection. There also are ways you can catch the attention of patrons of all ages right within the library itself. For instance, ask children to consider what they like most about a Newbery book they've read and have them draw, paint, or digitally create artwork that captures the essence of the book. Display the art on walls throughout the library for all to enjoy. This can help cultivate a sense of community within the library and demonstrates the imaginative activities going on over in the children's department.

Youth services advocacy does not have to be complicated. It can be a simple conversation with friends or a detailed presentation to community leaders. The key to advocacy is stories. Telling stakeholders the story of your library allows them to feel connected to the public institution. Sharing favorite childhood Newbery winners with friends, celebrating the YMAs with staff, polling patrons about their favorite winners, and sharing the excitement on social media can make a lasting impression on others and bring the library and its workers valuable support. The Newbery is a helpful tool in youth services advocacy. As the oldest, most well-known, and most respected award for children's literature, the Newbery highlights the importance of libraries. Without youth services librarians and staff, there would be no Newbery Award. Advocate for your position by reminding management, government agencies, and your community of the influence of the Newbery Award in the lives of patrons.

NOTE

1. For examples of how publishers and other professionals value the Newbery Award, see Shannon Maughan, "A Short History of the Newbery and Caldecott Medals," *Publishers Weekly*, December 2, 2011, www.publishersweekly.com/pw/by-topic/childrens/childrens-book-news/article/49729-and-the-winner-is.html; Jared S. Crossley, "A Chat with the Chair: 2021 Newbery Medal Chair Jonda C. McNair on Awards and Middle-Grade Books," The ALAN Review 49, no. 1 (Fall 2021); "Clemson Professor Appointed to Chair Prestigious Newbery Medal Committee," *Clemson News*, May 20, 2019, https://news.clemson.edu/clemson-professor-appointed-to-chair-prestigious-newbery-medal-committee/; Marty Crisp, "Newbery Boosts Careers, Expectations of Children's Authors," *LNP/LancasterOnline*, September 11, 2013, https://lancasteronline.com/news/newbery-boosts-careers-expectations-of-childrens-authors/article_3d41c15e-56be-5f91-a386-c99ebcce3ccc.html; Diane Roback, "Life after Newbery," *Publishers Weekly*, January 12, 2007, www.publishersweekly.com/pw/print/20070115/8129-life-after-newbery.html; and Lisa Fink, "100 Years of Newbery!" National Council of Teachers of English, November 14, 2021, https://ncte.org/blog/2021/11/100-years-newbery/.

Beyond the Book

ADDITIONAL RESOURCES/READINGS

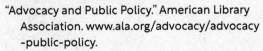

"Advocacy and Public Policy." American Library Association. www.ala.org/advocacy/advocacy-public-policy.

"ALSC Championing Children's Services Toolkit." ALSC Public Awareness Committee, 2019. www.ala.org/everyday-advocacy/speak-out/alsc-championing-childrens-services-toolkit.

Nemec-Loise, Jenna. "Spheres of Transformation." *Children and Libraries* 15, no. 2 (Summer 2017): 34–35. https://journals.ala.org/index.php/cal/article/view/6344.

"Public Awareness Tools and Resources." American Library Association. www.ala.org/advocacy/public-awareness/pr-tools.

CONCLUSION

The Enduring Value of the Newbery Award

JAMIE CAMPBELL NAIDOO

BOOKS HAVE THE POWER TO TRANSPORT READERS AND JUMPSTART CRE-
ativity. They can also reflect the social mores of the time, generally, and book
creators and publishers, specifically. Children's books that win high-profile literary awards, such as the Newbery, can hold considerable sway in the lives of
children and the adults who care about them. Noted children's literature edu-
cator and scholar Peggy Sullivan suggests that the Newbery Award "demands
the allegiance and attention of all who are concerned about children's literature."[1] While perhaps a bit zealous with her use of *allegiance*, Sullivan's com-
ment underscores the enduring value of Newbery Award-winning titles and
the important role these books play in the canon of children's books.

Throughout this volume numerous children's librarians and children's
literature scholars have critically examined various aspects of the Newbery
Award and provided suggestions for programming as well as advocacy. In this
conclusion, we will briefly explore the lasting influence that these books have
on readers, book creators, and caring adults who educate children in classrooms and libraries. But, first, allow me a short anecdote.

As a resourceful child growing up in rural Kentucky in the 1970s and '80s,
I found that stories provided an escape while also fanning the flames of my
imagination. I voraciously read books from both my public and school libraries, as well as the local bookmobile. It was in the collection of the latter that
I stumbled upon a magical book with a beautiful red and white cover—and
a gold sticker: Rachel Field's *Hitty, Her First Hundred Years*. I knew about gold
stickers on books from Ms. Beck, my elementary school librarian. A sticker
meant the book was important and had a good story. Written in 1929 and
recipient of the 1930 Newbery Award, *Hitty* follows the adventures of a small
wooden doll, carved in the 1800s, as she travels from Maine to various parts of

the world and then back to the United States, imparting bits of history along the way. As a child of about eight, I was fascinated with the idea that one of my dolls could have her own adventures without me. And, as a queer child who colored outside the gender lines with my toys, dress, and behavior, *Hitty* introduced me to male characters who treasured dolls as much as I did. After reading the book, I began scheming how I could make my own version of Hitty and the subsequent journeys we would take. With the help of *Childcraft: The How and Why Library* (1980 edition), I tried making a doll out of acorns and leaves and then out of wooden spoons. I never quite perfected my Hitty, but the creativity the book fostered led to hours of play and many more journeys to the library to find additional stories about dolls coming to life. For my younger self, this novel with a large gold seal succeeded as a Newbery book. As I will discuss later, as an adult, the book still holds value but not the same value that I placed on it as a child.

Give Me the Seal!: The Power of the Newbery Award

The mission of the ALSC is to engage library communities "to build healthy, successful futures for all children."[2] This is realized through the various professional resources, competencies, white papers, booklists, media awards, and other resources that the association offers. Many caregivers, educators, librarians, and researchers use the association's media awards to inform book selection for library collections, classroom libraries, and personal reading choices shared with children.

The gold seal of the Newbery Medal and the silver seal of the Honor serve as a stamp of approval that the book, whose cover bears the medal, is a high-quality piece of literature that has lasting value. Often these books are held as the gold standard in publishing, particularly by adults looking for the best in children's literature. When a title receives an award such as the Newbery, the book is almost guaranteed to find its way into the hands and hearts of readers both young and old, and to never go out of print.

Award-winning authors are likely to have increased success in the publication and sale of future work. Undeniably, an author's life changes almost instantly once they receive a Newbery Medal or Honor. Often their lives and previous works are catapulted into the spotlight. For some, this newfound prominence helps to get their important work into the hands of children who may have otherwise never encountered it. Too often it is assumed (whether overtly or covertly) by the publishing world, librarians, and educators that a book with a diverse character (or by a diverse author) is only for children from that cultural group.

In February 2015, librarian Amy Koester posted on The Show Me Librarian blog the entry "Selection Is Privilege" where she captures discussions from various librarian blogs and social media platforms about the problem of diversity in Newbery Award books. To be clear, this was not the problem related to a lack of diversity but a problem that there were too many diverse books selected for the 2014 Newbery. In essence, children's librarians suggested that books featuring diverse characters do not circulate well and that award committees should not select them. Koester's post shared her perspective that librarians, most of whom are white, unknowingly perpetuate white privilege in their selection process and reader's advisory on a daily basis by assuming that children only want to read books featuring their culture. She also observed that many librarians commented that because they do not have many children of color in their communities they should not have books representing racial diversity in their library collections.[3] The same has also been said about books with characters who are LGBTQIA+ (lesbian, gay, bisexual, transgender, queer, intersex, asexual, and more), disabled, non-Christian, and/or immigrant.

Books representing diverse characters hold value for *all* children. Yet, readers' lives are influenced when they see people like themselves or representing their culture winning the award, or books with characters "like them" receiving Newbery recognition. In essence, the sheer validation of identity shows that your culture matters, your people's stories matter, and you matter. But what happens when Newbery books fail to feature your culture, or depict it in stereotypical ways? Do these books have enduring value?

Teachable Moments and Social Justice Connections

Many Newbery Medal and Honor titles stand the test of time with engaging narratives, unforgettable characters, and beautiful language that resonate as much with contemporary children as their counterparts twenty-five, thirty-eight, or seventy years ago. However, not all award-winning titles age well. Sometimes technology or popular cultural references date a book, and other times the storylines present particular cultural groups in hurtful ways that perpetuate deep-seated stereotypes.

Let's return back to my childhood favorite, *Hitty*. About ten years ago, I decided to listen to an audio recording of the book. To say I was appalled is an understatement. I viscerally reacted, recoiling when I heard some of the language in the narrative. The book demeans people of different classes, cultures, and ethnicities; uses racial epithets; and includes broken English for persons of color, such as "I is gwine to tell you one thing an' dat is. . . ."[4] Hitty's xenophobic observations about characters, representing cultures divergent from her white American one, are extremely harmful when left unchecked. As a child, I did not comprehend these odious depictions of "the other" in the book. But, as an adult, I understand that by not addressing these problems with children, I am complicit in promoting the hurtful viewpoints of the author. It would be unconscionable for me as a librarian to recommend *Hitty* to a child who may not have caregiver support to challenge and question stereotypical depictions in the narrative.

Yet, Newbery books, such as *Hitty*, can offer enduring staying power and value by way of teachable moments that give children an opportunity to make social justice connections to the books. In her public service announcement for *PBS NewsHour*, Newbery Award-winning children's author-illustrator Grace Lin suggests that we treat problematic, "classic" children's books like "out-of-touch relatives."[5] We can appreciate them, but we must keep an ear out in case they offer an outdated message that is not consistent with our contemporary values of equity and inclusion. Librarians and other adults in the lives of children can share older Newbery titles with children and use them to talk about hurtful language, how this reinforces misunderstandings and stereotypes about a cultural group, to explore social injustices in the lives of readers, and to examine ways to avoid discrimination in larger society. While some adults suggest that classic books are just a sign of the times or a product of their original sociopolitical environment, it is our obligation as caring, informed adults to point out ways that specific titles demean particular cultural groups.

At the same time, Newbery titles like *Hitty* provide the opportunity to explore power dynamics over a period of time. Children's literature scholar Amy Singer observes, "Hitty's travels, both abroad and within different regions of the United States, and her hundred-year time frame add to her ability to provide a useful perspective on inequality, power, and social change. *Hitty* describes a social landscape that is constantly shifting, as emerging technologies and social experiences influence individual expectations."[6] In this instance, the actual narrative highlights social change and views. Given the book was written almost one hundred years ago, the ways cultural groups are depicted provide an equally compelling opportunity to examine perspective shifts on race, ethnicity, gender, and colonialism.

Although it might be tempting to suggest that older Newbery titles be updated for modern sensibilities to avoid harmful language, *Hitty* is the perfect case study of this problematic practice. In 1999 with the publication of *Rachel Field's Hitty: Her First Hundred Years*, Rosemary Wells adapted the text of Hitty with more contemporary language in some passages and removed problematic references to cultural groups. Illustrations were also added to make the book more appealing. Children's literature scholar Cathryn Mercier notes that "leaving out language that today's sensitive audience would find objectionable allows Susan Jeffers's illustrations not only to portray the shifting historical backgrounds across which Hitty traverses but also to depict what cannot now be said."[7] Yet, as Mercier observes, the adaptation causes the main character to lose her unique multidimensional voice and role as the book's authoritative narrator. At the same time, the modernization erases the built-in opportunity to explore shifts in representation and could be considered a form of censorship.

Rather than adapting problematic books or avoiding their use entirely with children, the best way to share older, dated Newbery titles is to pair them with their more modern counterparts. Then have children via individual or large group discussions compare and contrast the depiction of race, ethnicity, ability, or gender identity in titles from say 1942 and 2022. Librarians and other caregivers can scaffold conversations to explore harmful racial, ethnic, gender, and other cultural stereotypes. In doing so, this gives children the chance to examine why/how views have changed as well as to explore their own biases and discern ways to make a difference in their world to address microaggressions, injustice, and discrimination.

Looking Ahead: Reflections of All Children

One particular element that helps ensure the enduring value of a Newbery title is the author's ability to connect with a wide variety of children from diverse cultural backgrounds. Collectively, the most enduring Newbery books will be those that represent the rainbow of rich diversity in our culturally pluralistic society. Numerous studies have examined the representation of specific cultural groups in Newbery Medal and Honor Books.[8] The percentage of Newbery books with diverse characters or by diverse authors, while increasing in recent years, is still relatively low. To remain relevant, the awards should recognize more authors representing diverse gender identities, sexual orientations, disabilities, religious beliefs, ethnic identities, racial backgrounds, and more. At the same time, children deserve stories that capture their own unique cultural experiences while providing what Rudine Sims Bishop calls a window into the experiences of their cross-cultural counterparts.[9]

The power lies not only within the hands of the publishing world to publish more diverse books, but also in the decisions of future Newbery Award Selection Committees. When examining the Newbery Award at seventy-five, children's literature scholar Zena Sutherland noted that the medal and honor winners each year represent not only shifts in the publishing world but changes in the attitudes of the selection committees.[10] As the committee embraces the importance of culturally authentic, relevant stories, representing the lives of culturally pluralistic children, then more diverse winners will be selected. However, the impetus is on the formation of a diverse selection committee. One of the proudest moments during my year as ALSC president was a compliment that the Newbery Award Selection Committee I'd assembled was one of the most culturally diverse up to that point. This was reflected in the rich, diverse books selected that year to receive the Newbery Medal and Honor. Later, in 2022, all of the selected Newbery Medal and Honor Books represented titles written by diverse authors and featured culturally diverse characters. One 2022 Newbery title, Kyle Lukoff's *Too Bright to See*, broke new ground with Lukoff being the first openly transgender author to win a Newbery Honor and the book being the first Newbery title to have a main LGBTQIA+ protagonist—something that would have been unthinkable without shifts in social attitudes in both publishing and within the diverse selection committee.

As we look ahead to the next hundred years and beyond of the award, may we enjoy more enduring books that stand the test of time, reinforce the universality of experiences, and offer healthy, successful futures for all children. Yes, we might keep *Hitty* and other out-of-touch books to scaffold important conversations, but contemporary children deserve rich, relevant reflections of all children.

NOTES

1. Peggy Sullivan, "Victim of Success: A Closer Look at the Newbery Award," in *Issues in Children's Selection: A School Library Journal Anthology,* ed. *School Library Journal* (New York: R.R. Bowker Company, 1973), 32.

2. "About ALSC," ALSC, accessed September 21, 2021, www.ala.org/alsc/aboutalsc.

3. Amy Koester, "Selection Is Privilege," *The Show Me Librarian* (blog), February 8, 2015, http://showmelibrarian.blogspot.com/2015/02/selection-is-privilege.html#comment-form.

4. Rachel Field, *Hitty, Her First Hundred Years* (New York: Macmillan, 1929), 170.

5. Grace Lin, "What to Do When You Realize Classic Books from Your Childhood Are Racist," *PBS NewsHour,* August 11, 2017, www.pbs.org/newshour/show/realize-classic-books-childhood-racist.

6. Amy E. Singer, "A Novel Approach: The Sociology of Literature, Children's Books, and Social Inequality," *International Journal of Qualitative Methods* 10, no. 4 (2011): 317.

7. Cathryn Mercier, "Hitty Overboard," *The Horn Book Magazine* 76, no. 1 (2000): 108–09.

8. As an example, see Melanie Koss and Kathleen Paciga, "Diversity in Newbery Medal-Winning Titles: A Content Analysis," *Journal of Language and Literacy Education* 16, no. 2 (2020): 1–38; Melissa Leininger, Tina Taylor Dyches, Mary Anne Prater, and Melissa Allen Heath, "Newbery Award Winning Books 1975–2009: How Do They Portray Disabilities?," *Education and Training in Autism and Developmental Disabilities* 45, no. 4 (2010): 583–96; Cindy Gillespie, Janet Powell, Nancy Clements, and Rebecca Swearingen, "A Look at the Newbery Medal Books from a Multicultural Perspective," *The Reading Teacher* 48, no. 1 (1994): 40–50.

9. Rudine Sims Bishop, "Selecting Literature for a Multicultural Curriculum," in Using Multiethnic Literature in the K-8 Classroom, ed. Violet Harris (Norwood, MA: Christopher-Gordon Publishers, 1997), 1–20.

10. Zena Sutherland, "The Newbery at 75: Changing with the Times," *American Libraries* 28, no. 3 (1997): 34–36.

ABOUT THE CONTRIBUTORS

RAMONA CAPONEGRO, PhD, is the curator of the Baldwin Library of Historical Children's Literature at the University of Florida and a former professor of children's literature at Eastern Michigan University. She co-chaired the Pura Belpré Award 25th Anniversary task force and chaired the 2019 Pura Belpré Award Committee.

CASSIE CHENOWETH is a youth services librarian at Cobb County Public Library in Marietta, Georgia. She has served on ALSC's Public Awareness Committee and is the chair of the merged Public Awareness and Advocacy Committee. She can be contacted at cassie.chenoweth@gmail.com.

JARED S. CROSSLEY is a doctoral student specializing in children's and young adult literature in the College of Education and Human Ecology at The Ohio State University. A former elementary school teacher, he hopes to one day serve on the Newbery Award Selection Committee. He can be contacted at crossley.35@osu.edu.

DENISE DÁVILA, PhD, is an assistant professor of Children's Literature and Literacy Instruction at the University of Texas at Austin. Her current research agenda focuses on the development of family literacy and community partnership programs. One of her favorite children's books is *In My Family* by Carmen Lomas Garza.

ALPHA SELENE DELAP, PhD, is a library and media specialist and middle school advisor at the St. Thomas School in the greater Seattle area. At ALSC, she served on the Bechtel Fellowship Committee and the 2020 Newbery Award Selection Committee. She can be contacted at alpha.delap@stthomas school.org.

LORA DEWALT, PhD, serves Durham Public Schools as the director of teaching and learning. Her PhD from the University of Texas at Austin solidified her interest in researching children's literature, religious literacies, and literacy leadership. Her favorite children's book is *A Chair for My Mother* by Vera B. Williams.

STEVEN ENGELFRIED has been a librarian for thirty-five years, focusing on services to children. A member of the 2010 Newbery committee, he also chaired the 2013 committee. For the past five years, he has co-written the "Heavy Medal" Mock Newbery Blog for *School Library Journal*.

KIMBERLY PROBERT GRAD is a former school-age coordinator in the Youth and Family Services Department at Brooklyn (New York) Public Library. At ALSC, she served on the School Age Programs and Services Committee, the Newbery 100th Anniversary Celebration Task Force, and the 2022 Newbery Award Selection Committee. She is the director of the Abbot Public Library in Marblehead, Massachusetts.

JONDA C. MCNAIR is the Charlotte S. Huck Endowed Professor of Children's Literature at The Ohio State University. She specializes in books written by and about African Americans. A former elementary school teacher, she served as the chair of the 2021 Newbery Award Selection Committee. She can be contacted at mcnair.7@osu.edu.

JAMIE CAMPBELL NAIDOO, PhD, is the Foster-EBSCO professor and interim director at the University of Alabama School of Library and Information Studies. Naidoo was the 2018–19 president of ALSC and has served on the board of directors for both ALSC and the United States Board on Books for Young People (USBBY).

PAT R. SCALES is a retired middle and high school librarian and First Amendment advocate. She is a past president of ALSC and chaired the 1992 Newbery Award Selection Committee. She writes a bimonthly column, "Scales on Censorship," for *School Library Journal*.

MEGAN SCHLIESMAN is a librarian at the Cooperative Children's Book Center (CCBC), School of Education, University of Wisconsin-Madison. She manages the CCBC's Intellectual Freedom Information Services; provides reference services and presentations to Wisconsin librarians and teachers and university students about literature for youth; and reads and evaluates books for the library's annual best-of-the-year list, CCBC Choices.

INDEX

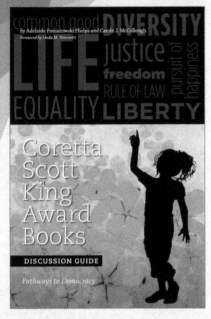